THE
BAGGY
GREEN

THE BAGGY GREEN

The pride, passion and history of Australia's sporting icon

MICHAEL FAHEY AND MIKE COWARD

A Gelding Street Press book
An imprint of Rockpool Publishing
PO Box 252
Summer Hill
NSW 2130 Australia

geldingstreetpress.com
Follow us! @ geldingstreet_press

Published in 2024 by Rockpool Publishing

Copyright text © Michael Fahey and Mike Coward 2024
Copyright design © Rockpool Publishing 2024

ISBN: 9781922662118

Cover design by Alissa Dinallo
Design and typesetting by Sara Lindberg, Rockpool Publishing
Publisher: Luke West, Rockpool Publishing
Edited by Lisa Macken
Cover images: (front) Newspix; (back, left to right) Alamy, Newspix, public domain

All rights reserved. No part of this publication may be reproduced, stored in a retrieval system, or transmitted in any form or by any means, electronic, mechanical, photocopying, recording or otherwise, without the prior written permission of the publisher.

 A catalogue record for this book is available from the National Library of Australia

Printed and bound in China
10 9 8 7 6 5 4 3 2 1

*For all those who aspire to wear the
precious baggy green cap.*

– Mike Coward

*To my wife Katie and family, thanks
for the support, guidance and patience
over the many years of research, writing
and speaking on the baggy green.*

– Michael Fahey

CONTENTS

Foreword: Mark Taylor		• ix
Foreword: Belinda Clark		• xiii
Introduction: The pride of the baggy green		• 1
1.	Captivated	• 5
2.	The road to the baggy green	• 31
3.	The gum-tree green and gold	• 43
4.	Collectors	• 65
5.	Values	• 77
6.	The Taj Mahal of baggy greens	• 93
7.	Variations and oddities	• 109
8.	Haddin's VB cap and the birth of Cricket Australia's cap	• 121
9.	Hats off to the women	• 129
10.	Capital appreciation	• 139
11.	One Test in time	• 153
12.	Wool promotions: from flock to baggy green	• 163
13.	Lap of honour	• 169
Endnotes		• 179
Acknowledgements		• 185
About the authors and contributors		• 189

Australian cricket captain Mark Taylor on the eve of his 100th Test milestone in November 1998. (Newspix)

FOREWORD

Mark Taylor

The baggy green cap is a powerful and timeless symbol that connects Victor Trumper to Pat Cummins.

A cricket cap is much more than part of a uniform. I have all my caps from the time I started playing in a team, and each one evokes precious memories of people, matches and moments. In a sense they are an archive. Being awarded a baggy green is the ultimate for a cricketer in Australia, and I am proud to have ensured the significance of this badge of honour is appreciated by everyone who loves the game in Australia and abroad.

Prior to a Test match in 1994 it was decided each member of the Australian team should wear the cap in the first session. The intention was to show off the beauty of the cap and our pride in it and not to intimidate our opponents, but there is no doubt its aura provides Australian teams with a psychological edge. There was never any intention to commercialise the cap or imply that the contemporary cricketer placed more importance upon it than his predecessors.

The baggy green is revered by everyone with a connection to Australian cricket, and this rich and revealing account of its history and rise to prominence is timely. It will be enthusiastically welcomed by those privileged to have worn the cap and, no doubt, by all those who dreamed of doing so.

Every cricketer who has represented Australia has made a priceless contribution to the history of the game. They are disparate characters who have served through good times and bad over 146 years, and they are bound together because they have worn with distinction the baggy green cap or its antecedent. More power to them, and may they long be recognised for their contribution to Australia's sporting and social history.

Mark Taylor, AO

Mark Taylor sweeps the ball to the boundary in England in 1997. (Alamy)

Australian captain Belinda Clark smashes a ball to the boundary during the Ashes Test at the Gabba in 2003. (Newspix)

FOREWORD

Belinda Clark

I was delighted to be asked to write a foreword for this new edition of *The Baggy Green*. It's wonderful that the evolution of the women's game has a place in the stories within this book about the baggy green cap.

When you grew up in a time when playing cricket was primarily the domain of brothers and fathers, what becomes important is simply the opportunity to play the game. It seemed a special occasion to have a hit in the nets, let alone play a real game, but as time passed and committed women kept advocating and organising the sport around kitchen tables and then board tables, the trajectory of the sport of cricket slowly started to change.

The symbols of the game are central to tracking the progress: they are the cricket grounds we play on, the heroes we admire, the honour boards and photos in the clubrooms and the uniforms we wear.

There were numerous critical steps in the women's game stepping up and announcing it was time to transform the sport in this country, but if we focus on the uniform then the first was the move from playing the sport in impractical culottes to pants that meant less skin was lost when athletic feats were performed. The second was the baggy green cap. This was not about the cap itself or what it represented to many Australians, including the males who had represented Australia, but rather the opportunity to connect the long line of women who since 1934–35 have proudly represented Australia.

The exercise to present every female player with a contemporary and now consistent version of the baggy green was one of the most rewarding and satisfying activities I have been involved in, as it effectively connected each and every one of the women who had played Test cricket. It is for this reason that my baggy green cap is on display in the Bradman Museum in Bowral, hopefully to spark interest in the journey of the women's game and inspire young girls and boys to follow their dreams.

Although for many of my contemporaries it was less about what you wore on your head and more about the chance to play, the symbol of the cap ties both the generations of female players and the sport together and ensures that we remember the foundations of the women's game.

Today's players are reaping the benefit of the pioneers from back in the early 20th century who ensured that the modern-day professional cricket system for women was possible. The system will not stand still and the evolution of the sport and its symbols will continue to evolve; however, I have a sneaking suspicion that the baggy green will remain among them.

Belinda Clark, AO

Belinda Clark enjoyed a long Test career from 1991 to 2005, captaining her country for much of that time. (Newspix)

Pat Cummins during the Ashes series launch in Brisbane in 2021. This was his first series as Australian captain. (Alamy)

INTRODUCTION

The pride of the baggy green

Cricket occupies a unique place in Australian sport: it was the first national game and remains so after almost 150 years of Test cricket. It is a game with a national side that significantly predates the Australian teams of all other major codes and even the Federation of the Australian colonies. Given this long pre-eminence, it is unusual that the national cricket team has not had either a name or logo that is marketed, especially in this brand-conscious era.

On the cricket field the only item of uniform that clearly identifies one side from another is the cap. The Australian Test cap is colloquially called the 'baggy green', and recently this term has sometimes been applied to the team and to cricket in Australia in general. Not registered until the beginning of the 21st century, by Australian cricket administrators, the term has come to be used by various commercial and non-commercial organisations. Baggygreen.com was operated by Nine MSN (now *Nine's Wide World of Sports*) and was the name of ESPNcricinfo's Australian website. Also, there was a cricket journal, *Baggy Green*, that was produced independently of Cricket Australia.

Although the Australian cap's nickname has come to be the name of cricket as a game and as a commercial activity in Australia, little is known about the cap's origins. Many, for instance, still believe the coat of arms on the cap is the official national coat of arms of the Australian government, but this is not the case. Even the Australian government's website Australia erroneously stated at one point: 'The Australian Government uses the coat of arms to authenticate documents and for other official purposes. Its uses range from embellishing the Australian passport to being widely recognised as the badge on the famous "baggy green" cricket cap.'[1]

Such misapprehensions have been accepted widely. The coat of arms on the Test cap predates Federation and the subsequent development of the official national coat of arms.

Although there has been no official marketing campaign, the extensive use of the name 'baggy green' and the wider appreciation of the cap have dramatically grown since the 1990s. Steve Waugh's attachment to his dilapidated cap is widely known, and it increased the appreciation of the cap as an icon that represents cricket at all levels while at the same time remaining a membership badge to a select club: Australian Test representatives, of which at the time of writing in November 2023 there were just 466 members. So renowned was the baggy green that in 2003 when Roger Knight, in his role as the Marylebone Cricket Club's chief executive, announced[2] a new relationship between the club and Albion, the maker of the baggy green cap, he said: 'We are delighted to be joining forces with a company of Albion's calibre. Its baggy green is the most famous cricket cap in the world.'[3]

Many people believe that the cap is so sacred an icon that it has never changed over the years. Again, this is not so: there have been many changes. The unravelling of the cap's history and its personal significance to players, public and collectors will help explain why the baggy green has been elevated to such a position of sporting and social esteem. The rise in the cap's profile is a threefold story.

First, the rise has been led by the players. Test captains such as Allan Border, Mark Taylor and Steve Waugh understood the cap's powerful symbolism for players and instituted a number of ceremonies and conventions designed to reinforce the cap's special place in the culture of the game.

Second, market forces have demanded the creation of brands, and the Australian Cricket Board – now Cricket Australia – embraced this with the creation of logos on shirts and sunhats. Throughout this process the administrators were determined not to commercialise the baggy green and to retain the original badge on the cap.

Third, the development of a commercial memorabilia market has increased the prestige of the baggy green cap. In Australia this market did not exist before 1993, but the marketing on the Nine Network of licensed products helped establish a revenue stream for the players, the Australian Cricketers' Association and the sport's governing body Cricket Australia. As well, the growth of the market for memorabilia meant that the exclusive group of serious collectors was exposed to a wider collecting market.

People have been selling or swapping cricketania for more than 120 years. However, for most of that time the market was based in England and required substantial research and good connections. New Australian money entered the English cricket memorabilia market in the late 1980s.[4] The success of Australian teams since the 1987 Cricket World Cup win and the 1989 Ashes victory meant that the market became global and the old system obsolete. Higher prices and greater demand meant the market expanded, and the extra exposure meant more items were valued rather than discarded or simply forgotten.

What we now call the 'baggy green' has taken many forms. (Image courtesy of Michael Fahey)

Later in this book we examine the reactions of former and current Australian players to the iconic status of the baggy green cap. We also explore the media hype and high prices surrounding various Bradman cap auctions and acquisitions, and how these developments fit into the history of the baggy green cap. Finally, we explore the unique story of the women's baggy green and see if there is relevance still for the cap and its traditions some 15 years since this book's first publication.

MF

Michael Clarke celebrates his maiden Test century by kissing his baggy green in Bangalore, India in October 2004. (Newspix)

CHAPTER 1

Captivated

The romancing of the baggy green was so pervasive by October 2004 that future Australian captain Michael Clarke discarded his helmet and called for his brand-new cap as he drew within two runs of a century in his first Test innings. For a 23-year-old greenhorn with a rudimentary knowledge of his illustrious predecessors and the game's history it was a powerful and symbolic act that soon became a part of the rich lore of Australian cricket. Clarke reasoned it would be tantamount to irreverence to realise his greatest dream wearing and waving a helmet and not his iconic baggy green cap 389.

The rituals honouring and saluting the baggy green continued to grow over the next 19 years as 77 players were inducted into the ultimate Australian cricket brethren. By the time Matthew Kuhnemann received cap 466 from Marnus Labuschagne, a close mate and fiercely proud holder of cap 455, the observance was a profound rite.

Labuschagne was an eight-year-old immigrant from South Africa learning English and the vernacular of Australian cricket when Clarke made his grand gesture at the M. Chinnaswamy Stadium in Bangalore, yet 15 years later it was he who emotionally flourished his helmet to acknowledge the applause of his adopted home crowd at the Gabba for his maiden Test century against Pakistan. 'I don't think I would have been game enough to take off my helmet on 98,' pondered Labuschagne, who is as passionate about the baggy green as anyone breastfed in Australia and raised on tales about Trumper, Bradman, the Chappells, Border and the Waughs.

Just as Clarke's dreams of Test selection intensified when he reached the first-class arena at age 18, Labuschagne at 20 was consumed by thoughts of a higher calling when Martin Love, protector of baggy green 385, presented him with his Queensland cap in 2014. Like the celebrated players before them and those destined to follow, Clarke and Labuschagne were engulfed by waves of raw emotion as they fulfilled boyhood dreams of a Test match century.

'I would like to have held on to that moment for longer, to remember what the feeling was like,' Clarke said. He was, however, numbed and to this day has no recollection of who brought the cap to him in the middle and what, if anything, was said. He knows it was presented to him before the match by Shane Warne but guiltily confesses to not remembering a word his good friend said in commendation and congratulation. Such was his trance-like state he simply stared at the cap through tears.

Conversely, Labuschagne remembers exactly the words Mike Hussey carefully chose when presenting him with his cap before his first Test in Dubai in the United Arab Emirates the second week of October 2018. 'His wise words still stick with me,' Labuschagne said. 'After telling me what an honour it was to play for Australia, he said it would be the way I dealt with pressure that would define me as a player.' Given the supreme challenge Labuschagne faced as Test cricket's first full substitute against England fast bowler Jofra Archer at Lord's 10 months later, it was the most prescient observation.

Five years later in the smog of the Indian capital Delhi, Labuschagne was untroubled to find the appropriate words and sentiment when he presented cap 466 to Kuhnemann. 'It was a real privilege to present the cap to my mate and share such a special moment,' Labuschagne said. 'In a way, the cap means even more away from home because you are seen as an ambassador.'

While a raised and kissed helmet has become an increasingly familiar response to the acclaim of crowds since the late 1970s, it is the doffing of the cap that maintains tradition and evokes memories of the greatest batsmen and their finest deeds. By holding aloft his cap, Clarke also effectively paid homage to the 11 other Australians who announced their brilliance with 100 in their first Test innings: a disparate band headed by Charles Bannerman, who amassed an undefeated 165 in the first Test in March 1877. While Bannerman wore a cap of a different style and colour, the legendary quartet of Bill Ponsford, Archie Jackson, Doug Walters and Greg Chappell accomplished the feat in the name of the baggy green during a 45-year period and before the helmet was refined and became de rigueur.

The baggy green cap has become a centrepiece of Australia's vibrant cricket history. It is the one constant, a reassuring reference point in a game that is forever changing and has done so at disconcerting speed since the World Series Cricket schism of 1977 to 1979.

The modern masters are proud at being imbued with the spirit of the past, and Clarke's triumph effectively linked the events in 2004 at the M. Chinnaswamy Stadium in the garden city of India and the first Test at Melbourne in the garden state of Victoria 127 years earlier. That this connection was made and highlighted in the media gladdened the hearts of Mark Taylor and Steve Waugh, Australia's Test match captains from September 1994 to January 2004, and justified their earnest endeavours to ensure the first elite cricketers of the 21st century were aware of the identity and deeds of those who had gone before them.

Their immediate predecessors, Allan Border and Kim Hughes, on the spur of the moment used the cap as a psychological prop when facing heavy defeat but went unrewarded. Confronting an innings defeat against the West Indies in Antigua in April 1984, Hughes asked all his men to wear the cap at the death in an admirable but forlorn show of defiance and pride.

It has been said and written that the Australian team in dire straits against New Zealand in Auckland in March 1993 acted in the same way while nearing a five-wicket defeat, but skipper Border had no recollection of making a formal directive. Providentially, Taylor was in the team, and he felt strongly that more attention needed to be paid to the significance of the cap and greater efforts made to distinguish it from the flotsam and jetsam associated with the modern game.

When he began his Test career against the West Indies in 1988 Taylor received his baggy green in a metre-square cardboard box. At least the cap was on top of the training shirts and jumpers. Four years earlier Dean

Jones opened the package sent to the family home at Mount Waverley in Victoria and needed to dig deep through shirts and long and sleeveless jumpers to find his precious cap at the bottom of the pile.

Kim Hughes, holding a stump after winning the Ashes in 1983, felt that the cap and blazer were neither worn nor respected when he entered the international arena around the time of World Series Cricket. (Newspix)

Bob Merriman, a distinguished administrator who managed Australian teams to India, England, New Zealand and Sharjah in the United Arab Emirates in the 1970s and 1980s before rising to be chairman of Cricket Australia, vividly recalled Australian Cricket Board secretary Alan Barnes distributing caps to Kim Hughes's team to India in 1979 as though he was delivering newspapers from a moving vehicle. The caps were tossed across a room.

It was such an absence of ceremony that disappointed Taylor, who had fond memories of the ritual guernsey presentation nights at his Tigers Australian football club at Wagga Wagga in his youth. Two years after succeeding Allan Border as captain and insisting each member of the team wear the baggy green cap for the first session of the first Test match with England at the Gabba in November 1994, Taylor instituted a formal cap presentation. Before the first Test with the West Indies in Brisbane in November 1996 he called his men together and chose his words carefully as he presented caps to Michael Kasprowicz and Matthew Elliott.

For Kasprowicz, a genial, lion-hearted pace bowler who gave yeoman service for the next decade, the formal presentation of the cap brought another unforgettable dimension to his debut before his home crowd. 'The celebration of the cap is a good idea – it is something special because the game is so rich and steeped in history,' Kasprowicz said. 'In these changing times of Twenty20, graphite strips on bats and different rules changes the baggy green represents constancy. It is a constant and that's the beauty of it.

'The cap is a special part of you – almost like a tattoo. You only realise the power of it when you are in and out of the team. I always try and capture the moment in case it is the last time I play or share the dressing room. I never take it for granted.'

Kasprowicz's analogous use of the word 'tattoo' is appropriate. Among his peers, Colin Miller marked his brief but fascinating 18-match mid-life Test career with an image of the baggy green tattooed on a buttock. Michael Slater, Mark Waugh, Michael Clarke and Ricky Ponting have had their Test cum cap number tattooed on various parts of their bodies, Clarke's 389 boldly in Roman numerals across the small of his back. 'You only scar your body for something precious,' Clarke said.

Steve Waugh brought another dimension to subsequent cap presentation ceremonies after he took over the captaincy in the West Indies in 1999. To mark the induction of Adam Gilchrist and Scott Muller into the team for the first Test with Pakistan in the summer of 1999–2000 he called upon Bill Brown to present their caps and so welcome them into the family of Australian Test cricketers. Brown, a former Australian captain and member of Don Bradman's legendary Invincibles to England in 1948, said he was immensely proud to be involved in such a presentation 65 years after receiving his first baggy green to very little fanfare at Nottingham in England.

Bill Brown in England during the 1934 Ashes tour, the first of three tours to England. (Alamy)

When Bill Brown died aged 95 in March 2008, Steve Waugh told *The Courier-Mail*: 'I reckon that if one person could have their picture inside the baggy green cap to illustrate what it stood for, it should be Bill. Bill was the man who my generation really looked up to. For us he was the embodiment of everything great about the baggy green cap. He had everything – strength, great ethics, character and wonderful stories from the past and yet had great respect for the modern game.'

This affable soul so beloved by Australia's contemporary players was bemused at the importance placed upon the cap and the commercial value that had been ascribed to it since the early 1990s. 'In my day they were just cricket caps and flung into our bags,' Brown said in late 2007. 'They were just part of the attire and not regarded much higher than your boots and treated much the same. We didn't look after them. Undoubtedly, if I had my time over again I would treat them with greater care. I'm sorry now, but it was my fault,' Brown added.

Brown didn't have a cap in his collection of memorabilia at his Brisbane home. Like so many players down the years he gave his caps away, and he smiles at the recollection of a grandchild wearing one of his baggy greens to a Sunday school picnic. Throughout his phenomenal career Gilchrist felt a special bond with the indefatigable Brown and always looked forward to meeting him on the cricket circuit.

That the baggy green is now widely seen as an embodiment of the spirit and history of Australian cricket and not merely as part of the playing uniform is one of the greatest legacies of the mightily successful Taylor–Waugh era. Allan Border, who so gallantly constructed the platform from which Taylor and Steve Waugh continued to advance Australia fair, fervently believes the rest of the cricket world is deeply jealous of the awesome power the cap engenders.

'I think it is fantastic that the baggy green has this iconic status,' Border said. 'The aura and historical significance of the cap gives Australian teams a psychological advantage. Other teams may be proud of their cap but don't talk about it with the same passion. By all wearing the cap in the first session it has an aura and the team is making a statement. Steve Waugh deserves much credit for initiating or rekindling the spirit of the baggy green. He has given it great focus. It is a tremendous legacy.'

Steve Waugh, whose voice was said to be the loudest at the memorable team meeting in Brisbane in 1994 that led to all 11 members of the team wearing the baggy green in the first session, played on for five years after Taylor retired at the age of 34 at the end of the 1998–99 international summer. By the time he bade an emotional farewell against India in the first week of January 2004, Waugh was within six months of his 39th birthday and any image of him without his battered but beloved baggy green seemed incomplete and inappropriate.

Waugh and his cap were inseparable as the Australian people rose to him. His deep affection for the traditional game and its lustrous history and timeless values and virtues never blunted his enthusiasm for the frenetic and often crudely played and marketed limited-overs game. Together with thrilling extrovert batsman Dean Jones he was an unabashed fan and promoter of compressed cricket, and it was his phenomenal all-round exploits at the 1987 World Cup on the Indian subcontinent that largely forged his cricket persona and earned him the sobriquet of 'Iceman'.

When the Australian selectors controversially decided to differentiate between five-day and one-day cricket for the summer of 1997–98, Waugh was appointed captain for limited-overs matches and Taylor remained at the helm in Test matches. While the one-day game has enormous appeal to spectators, especially women, adolescents and children it is considered an amusing and lucrative distraction by the vast majority of elite players, who judge their peers on their ability in the traditional arena. Critics, too, hold a similar view.

While he was as anxious as Taylor to lift the profile of the baggy green and draw public attention to the significance of a player's designated place in his history of the game, Waugh was concerned specialist one-day players could be overlooked by contemporaries, commentators and, indeed, by history. This concern prompted him to suggest the Australian one-day squad wear their allocated numbers on their coloured caps during the triumphant 1999 World Cup campaign in England and Wales. Waugh felt strongly that it would provide the team with a sense of belonging. It was not, however, an initiative that could be acted upon at a moment's notice after an often-fraught, tied Test tour of the West Indies.

Ever the lateral thinker, Waugh sought the help and local knowledge of his genial all-rounder and one-day specialist Tom Moody, who continued to win impressive notices for his leadership of Worcestershire in English county cricket. Before the opening match against Scotland at the picturesque Worcester ground, Waugh and Moody thumbed through the yellow pages of regional telephone directories and eventually reached an affable grandmother who assured them she could produce the numbers required for embroidering onto each of the 15 Australian players' two caps. It was as well she lived in Cardiff, where Australia was to play New Zealand

Neil Harvey, who played 79 Tests from 1948 to 1963, was mostly bare-headed on the field. (Newspix)

in their second match. In the end the senior seamstress's work, completed in just two days, was a little too bold and Waugh opted for an alternative.

Because of this initiative by Waugh England's Test players wore their designated number on their shirts for the Ashes series of 2001, and Waugh ensured that the Australians followed suit against New Zealand and South Africa in 2001–02.

While Waugh's cap is among the most venerated items of Australian cricketania, it is not the only baggy green Waugh donned in his remarkable career – nor is it clear if it is the cap that was presented on his debut against India at Melbourne in December 1985. Waugh had long believed and recorded in his autobiography that his celebrated cap was the first he ever received as a member of the Australian under-19 team that played Pakistan in 1984. This team, which also included his twin brother Mark and Mark Taylor, was indeed furnished with baggy greens, but they were emblazoned with 'Youth XI'. Furthermore, he played in another cap in England in 1993, having misplaced – temporarily as it happened – the cap in use in the summer of 1992–93. He played in at least two and in all

Mark Taylor (right) wearing his baggy green celebrates the 1998 Ashes win with Ian Healy in cap and Mark Waugh in floppy. (Alamy)

probability three, which is scarcely surprising given that his Test career spanned a tad more than 18 years.

Conversely, Taylor, who often favoured a white floppy hat because of fears he was susceptible to skin cancers, is convinced he used just one baggy green throughout his 10-year, 104-Test career. That he has two others in pristine condition bespeaks the generosity of spirit of Lawrie Sawle, one of the great servants of Australian cricket, who managed Taylor's triumphant party to the Caribbean in 1995. Justin Langer is perhaps the only other long-serving player of this spectacularly successful period who can lay claim to using just the one cap for more than 100 Test matches, and he quipped at his valedictory press conference at the close of the 2006–07 Ashes series that its stench was such it would need to be housed behind thick glass. Certainly, at least David Boon, Adam Gilchrist and Ricky Ponting for one reason or another used two caps.

Ponting, the 42nd Australian captain, was inspired by the philosophy of Waugh and Taylor, under whom he made his debut as a 20 year old in 1995, and as he grew in confidence at the helm was keen to maintain and build on the traditions. Very much his own man, he wasted little time in discarding the garish Harlequin blazers that to his dismay had been favoured for a period. As far as he was concerned these had no connection with the traditions of Australian cricket. He had them replaced with a striking green blazer with gold piping fashioned after that worn by Don Bradman during his period as captain from 1936 to 1948.

As intent as his immediate predecessors to make a lasting contribution to the livery of the Australian team, Ponting had number 42 embroidered into the pocket of his blazer. At the start of the 2007–08 season he even pondered the wisdom of introducing specific caps to identify the captain and those privileged to have played in 100 or more Test matches.

Ponting never wore anything other than the baggy green, and with the emphatic support of his deputy Adam Gilchrist he urged all players to wear it at all times. Those reluctant to conform such as Shane Warne and Mark Waugh were regularly if gently taunted by the leadership group. Ponting made no apology for this; indeed, he even liked his men to wear the cap at the start of a fielding session and insisted it be compulsorily worn at victory celebrations that culminated with the intoning of the team anthem. At Ponting's direction such flannelled corroborees have taken place atop Table Mountain at Cape Town in South Africa and at the spectacular ancient Galle Fort in Sri Lanka.

At these intimate gatherings sponsors' caps are removed and the baggy green worn. This ritual seems to have had its genesis at Manchester when Allan Border's team so famously regained the Ashes in 1989. After the initial champagne and beer swilling and spraying celebration in the dressing room, David Boon and his close pal Geoff Marsh walked to their coffins and put on their caps. It was unrehearsed and further stirred emotions in the dressing room: it just seemed the right thing to do. Ponting, like Taylor and Waugh before him, believed the uniform wearing of the baggy green in the first session of a Test match was a compelling aesthetic that provided the Australians with an aura and thus a competitive edge. He made certain his younger charges, Michael Clarke in particular, were cognisant of their responsibilities to the baggy green and to the exclusive band of men who have worn it. 'I have the ultimate respect for the cap and if I have any input into the next generation I will see the tradition continues,' Clarke declared.

Australian players celebrate winning against the West Indies in 2000. Justin Langer pours beer on the caps of teammates. (Newspix)

Vivid memories of the awesome 1980s West Indians, men who seemed as tall, strong and immovable as the palm tree on their caps, prompted Steve Waugh to discuss the matter at the team meeting in Brisbane in 1994. He felt strongly that along with the swagger the cap had provided the West Indians with a unity of purpose and an air of invincibility, and it was something he wanted the Australians to emulate. However, as far as skipper Taylor was concerned the decision for all 11 players to wear the cap onto the Gabba at the start of the Ashes series was made in the name of aesthetics. 'It was not designed to scare the opposition. It was designed to look good for the side,' Taylor said.

Whether such regimentation has ever unsettled opposition is debatable. Richie Benaud is sure Don Bradman once told him he had used the ploy in England in 1948 but this could not be corroborated by Sam Loxton and Arthur Morris, members of Bradman's Invincibles.

The baggy green elicits a multiplicity of emotions and attitudes from those privileged to have worn it. Without exception these men, famous and forgotten, speak of a profound sense of pride and privilege. Some talk of the humbling nature of attaining it, others of an awesome responsibility to justify selection and serve the ghosts of long-gone summers. There are those who speak unself-consciously of a reverence for the cap and those who foresee dangers in its worship. Some, former captain Bob Simpson among them, contend it should be worn only in pristine condition and abhor the contemporary practice of wearing the cap to the point of its disintegration. 'Utter nonsense!' counter others who have guarded their cap with their sporting life.

While the intrinsic value of the baggy green has always been appreciated, its commercial worth and desirability to collectors and investors is a consequence of the cap culture developed by Taylor and Waugh. Indeed, Simpson and fast bowler Frank Misson are among those who attest to the fact that in the 1950s and 1960s the baggy green was never referred to as such. It was a cap and nothing more than a cap, an item of apparel in their kit or canvas bag, and that is where it generally stayed between matches. It was respected for it had long been coveted, but it was never idolised.

'In 1961 there was not the depth of emotion associated with the cap,' Misson said. 'It was referred to as the "cap" and not the "baggy green" and, if anything, there was more emphasis on the romance of the colours of green and gold. There was probably a feeling that the cap was a little unfashionable. Most other countries had a baseball or skullcap. Certainly ours was more flouncy. I think there was a thought it was a bit old-fashioned and the [caps of the] other countries looked a little more sartorial.'

As rumbustious fast bowler Jeff Thomson observed with customary succinctness: 'The main thing was to be in the team. It had nothing to do with the cap. Even if I had nothing I'd know I'd played for Australia.' Bill Lawry concurred: 'The cap was nice but it was the honour of playing that meant most, be it for club, state or country.'

By the time Waugh had retired in 2004, Taylor recognised that the new culture of the baggy green and the inevitable media and auction house emphasis on its steadily increasing dollar value had polarised a good number of former Australian players. 'My intention was never to commercialise the baggy green,' Taylor said. 'It disappoints me a little that it has become a commercial item rather than a personal one. I would hate to think that players would look to it as an investment. I'm sure this is not the case.

Doug Walters (right), here with one of his closest mates, Ian Chappell, often reflects on the trend during his era of predominantly wearing the white floppy hat. (Newspix)

'I am concerned that it might seem to make the players of today more valuable than the players of the past. That is certainly not the case. I wanted to make the cap something special and keep it apart from the paraphernalia. There is just so much stuff that I didn't want the baggy green to get lost. That I have played a small part in making the baggy green such a strong and recognisable national symbol makes me very proud.'

Many of Taylor's predecessors are among those with the greatest reservations about the wider community's fascination with the baggy green and the monetary value now attached to it. 'I say this not in a derogatory way, but it has only been in recent times there has been this kerfuffle about the baggy green,' Richie Benaud said. 'There used not to be anyone beating their breast or talking about the baggy green. And no one was spraying beer over it. I was proud of playing for Australia and I don't feel any different about the Australian cap as I did when I was playing and captain. It is a piece of memorabilia and I've never been a memorabilia person.'

Other than photographs of a special gathering of Australian captains in Brisbane, Allan Border's triumphant Australians at Old Trafford in 1989 and a splendid image of the Sydney Cricket Ground in 1880 given to him by Ian and Barbara Chappell, Benaud had little cricket memorabilia at his home at the beachside suburb of Coogee in Sydney.

Benaud long dined out on the fact that one of his baggy green caps bought for 50 cents at an opportunity shop at Dee Why on Sydney's northern beaches sold for $10,925 the day a Bradman bat fetched $33,200 at auction. While he wore his cap in his first Test against the West Indies in January 1952 and for much of the following summer against South Africa, for the rest of his distinguished 63-Test career to February 1964 Benaud was, much like his faithful deputy Neil Harvey, mostly bareheaded in the middle whether batting or fielding.

Bill Lawry, who made his Test debut under Benaud in 1961 and was destined to succeed Bob Simpson as captain in 1967, simply noted: 'These are different times and there is now a commercial value rather than a sentimental value attached to the baggy green.' However, it is Ian Chappell, who followed Lawry at the helm in February 1971, who is characteristically strident. 'There's only one way you get a slouch hat and one way you get a baggy green. You play or you fought,' Chappell said, 'and I would never wear a slouch hat because I never fought. A lot of what goes on with the baggy green is for commercial reasons and I have a major problem with that.' Like Benaud, Chappell does not possess a baggy green cap other than the miniature that was presented along with a plaque declaring each player's designated place in batting order since 15 March 1877. Chappelli is number 231.

'Playing for Australia was really important, not the cap. I don't ever remember having one discussion about the cap during my playing days,' Chappell stated. He also can't recall his famous grandfather Vic Richardson ever playfully placing a baggy green on his head as he netted with Chappell's brothers Greg and Trevor in the backyard of the family home at North Glenelg in Adelaide.

Richardson, who played 19 Test matches and led Australia to a spectacular 4–0 success against South Africa in 1935–36, never drew attention to his accomplishments and kept his baggy green at the bottom of the canvas bag that found its way to the Chappell household. The boys were much more interested in the bats, balls and baseball gloves with which they could play. While he was proud to have earned his baggy green, Chappell considered it only another item of apparel and, much like his grandfather, disliked ostentatious displays of the cap.

Widely acknowledged as one of the game's most inspirational leaders, Chappell's forthright if not bolshy approach to aspects of the captaincy alienated the game's conservative governors, with whom he was often in conflict. He captained Australia throughout the 1970s to a backcloth of social restlessness and non-conformity, and the casualness in dress – floppy white hats were in vogue – and demeanour of his men earned them the unwanted label of the 'Ugly Australians'. Be that as it may, they were much loved by the Australian people, and nearly 40 years later the leading lights of the Chappell era still occupy a special place in the hearts and minds of the Australian cricket community.

That the baggy green was not uniformly worn through this period was interpreted by many as an anti-establishment gesture by Chappell and the revolutionaries at his command. To a man they were tired of being treated as serfs by the masters in mahogany row at the Australian Cricket Board and sought drastic changes to every aspect of the game. By 1977 the winds of change had gathered cyclonic velocity.

So pervasive was the anti-establishment sentiment that John Inverarity, who toured England in 1968 and 1972 and for a short time was deputy to Chappell, felt out of place if he wore cap and blazer. 'At Arundel [for the traditional one-day Ashes tour opener] I put my cap on because it was an opportunity to do so,' Inverarity said. 'Then I realised I was the only one who was capped and so proud to be so. At the same time I was aware that such an expression of this pride was infra dig. I felt a little self-conscious but felt I wasn't in a position to share that thought for it was a little too earnest or conscientious.'

Kim Hughes, who ultimately captained his country, experienced similar feelings of alienation. Hughes, 10 years younger than Inverarity and a fellow Western Australian, felt that the cap and blazer were neither worn nor respected when he entered the international arena at the very

Warne in floppy leaves the MCG for the last time in 2006 with a stump and match ball as mementos. (Newspix)

time the startling details of the World Series Cricket upheaval were reaching the public domain.

'I wanted to sleep in my cap, I was so excited,' observed Hughes, who at the age of 23 was chosen for the final Test in England in 1977 under the captaincy of Greg Chappell. 'I had worked so hard for it, [as] had my parents and my coach. And it wasn't required. I found that awkward but it was the times – the time of anti-establishment feelings.'

Greg Chappell's view of the baggy green was starkly different to his older brother's, and in 2007–08 he kept one in storage as he flitted about the world meeting commercial commitments that arose primarily as a result of his tumultuous two-year stint as coach of the Indian cricket team. 'The cap was always important to me but not in the way it has become today. It was always something special to pull it on and I was always aware of the history and what had gone before. It might not have been the focus of so much as it is today but it was certainly a powerful symbol.'

Shane Warne and Mark Waugh in their customary white floppies at the 2001 Boxing Day Test at the MCG. (Newspix)

Doug Walters, one of Ian Chappell's closest mates, conceded that he often reflects on the aberration of predominantly wearing the white floppy hat. 'I didn't wear the cap much at all. We wore the white floppies. I don't know why, really. It was a stupid trend. Why would you wear the floppy when you could wear the cap?' he asked almost plaintively. 'The baggy green was something I dreamed of getting as a kid. I knew that was the ultimate and I told my school teachers I didn't have to do homework because I would play Test cricket for Australia and wear the baggy green. They dismissed such a notion but I proved them wrong.'

A renowned raconteur, Walters donated the bulk of his caps to various charitable causes over many years but cherishes his first baggy presented before he became just the fifth Australian to score a century in his first Test innings: a glorious 155 against England at Brisbane in December 1965. That more than 25 years after his retirement from Test cricket Walters laments not wearing his cap more often is indicative of the renewed respect afforded the baggy green since Taylor and Waugh devised means to add to its lustre.

Respect for the cap and its lustre in the most literal sense is an issue that polarises those who have served the baggy green. Steve Waugh in particular was widely criticised and even condemned in some quarters for wearing his famous cap in a decrepit state. His contemporaries, most notably Justin Langer, defended him vigorously, but seeing a dilapidated baggy green publicly paraded has irritated a host of former players.

Geoff Lawson, who played alongside Waugh in 10 Test matches between November 1986 and December 1989, was most annoyed. 'I certainly have not liked the fact that Steve Waugh wore his baggy green until it had fallen apart,' Lawson said. 'I thought that disrespectful. It looked tatty and neglectful. I'm not quite sure what his aim was, but it was disrespectful not respectful.'

Keith Stackpole, who played 43 times for Australia and for a period was vice-captain to Ian Chappell, was well known for his strident observations as a radio and newspaper critic since he retired from the first-class arena in 1973–74. 'I see faded caps, caps out of shape, and I don't like it,' he observed. 'Caps are meant to be worn in pristine condition.

'I don't go along with all this nonsense about the baggy green cap. I don't like the way it has gone. It's purely commercial and has gone over the top. We used to have a fitting for the cap – now there is elastic on the side. I think the cap would have meant more in the old days when they batted in them. I can't understand why they mean that much when they don't bat in the things. In the old days players would practise in them too, but not now.'

Stackpole and the baggy green were not a natural fit. While his heart swelled with pride at the honour of representing his country, he found the plastic in the centre of the cap lining caused him to sweat profusely.

He even pondered whether the constant and intense head sweating contributed to the melanoma on his scalp he had to battle later in life. Coincidentally, his protégé Dean Jones complained that the cap constantly gave him headaches.

Colin McDonald and Bob Simpson, who opened the batting in four of the five Tests of the epic series with the West Indies in 1960–61, expressed concerns at trends evident in the contemporary game. McDonald, who played 47 Tests between 1952 and 1961 (14 with Simpson), recalled that 'baggy green' was a part of the game's lexicon when he began his Test career alongside Richie Benaud and George Thoms in 1952. 'I'm all for the fact it has such status now, that it is an iconic item of memorabilia,' he said.

'I'm pleased it has this status and that the current players value it so highly. But I was disappointed when Steve Waugh and others wore the cap in such a dilapidated state. It was a shame he did that. I don't think he realised how dreadful it looked. Perhaps Cricket Australia should set down a rule that they have to be changed periodically to guard against dilapidation. It is important to maintain the look and image of such a prestigious item.'

Simpson agreed: 'I'm disappointed in the way the cap looks nowadays. It has been denigrated a bit and looks bad on the modern player. Wearing them for so long probably has come about because of superstition, but it suggests a lack of respect. Be assured the cap earned great respect and it made a big difference overseas and was talked about because it was so different from the others, but to make a full impact and be seen at its best it must be in pristine condition. It was unsaid but understood that the cap was to be worn in pristine condition.'

Ross Edwards, a gritty middle-order batsman and glorious cover fieldsman in 20 Tests in the 1970s, believed that superstition will have wittingly or unwittingly contributed to the fashion of wearing the cap to the point of its disintegration. 'It has partly to do with the fact that cricketers are superstitious. If you get runs in a cap you wear it. I'm not sure whether you should tour with a crappy old cap. That's the individual's choice. I couldn't do that. But if you had a cap and you weren't getting runs in it, it would be a temptation to go back to the one from the past.'

Justin Langer, the most loyal of Steve Waugh's acolytes, was irritated beyond measure at the carping directed at his guru for wearing a badly frayed baggy green. In his book *The Power of Passion* (Gary Allen Pty Ltd, 2002) he wrote: 'As far as I am concerned these people mustn't have anything better to talk about. Like the martial arts master, Steve Waugh's cap is symbolic of everything that is great about Steve Waugh and Australian cricket.'

In recent years the term 'baggy green' has found its way into the index of the memoirs of some contemporary players. This is a far cry from the reference to the subheading of 'Cap' under 'Equipment' in Don Bradman's famous text of 1958, *The Art of Cricket* (Hodder & Stoughton, 1958). He wrote: 'Unless the weather is dull, I think it advisable to wear a cap. I have seen more than one player affected by the sun in hot climates and I have also seen many catches missed by capless players who would certainly have had a better chance of seeing the ball with a cap on.'

Justin Langer in his beloved baggy green poses with the Australian mascot Schkimpy in 2001. (Alamy)

Brian Booth, an admired Christian gentleman, mentor and educationist who represented Australia at both hockey and cricket, had deep respect for the baggy green but warned against its glorification: 'The commercialisation of the caps doesn't faze me but I am uneasy about the idol worship. I certainly don't bow down to them.' Booth twice deputised for his injured and ill skipper Bob Simpson during the 1965–66 Ashes series. Jeff Thomson is of like mind: 'Of course it means something to get one but I'm not one to sit around and kiss the cap and blazer. Anyway, they didn't have the value when I was playing. They could be replaced and were often swapped.' His great pal Len Pascoe found a baggy green lying in the dressing room at the end of a day's play at Lord's in 1977: none of his teammates ever claimed it.

Such is the aura of the baggy green that initially it can overwhelm and even intimidate the recipient. 'I can recall when I first received the cap sitting in my room and holding it and wondering whether I was worthy of it,' David Boon said. 'The cap is the tangible representation of the privilege of playing for Australia. Everything is represented by the cap. I valued it more as my career unfolded and you keep it on your head for as long as you can. And when you no longer wear it, it is sacred.'

Pascoe vividly remembered being consumed by self-doubt as Greg Chappell's Ashes party winged its way to England in 1977. 'I confessed to Max Walker that I just didn't know if I was good enough,' he said. 'Max told me that when I had the baggy green on my head I would be the best my country would offer and I would play as it was meant to be. He said: "You will have a sense of security, you will have the history of the cap and its traditions and it will give you the confidence to be the best you can be. This is the essence of the baggy green."'

Pascoe played 14 Test matches and had the distinction of sharing the attack with his great pal Thomson, the incomparable Dennis Lillee as well as his guide Walker. He shared the new ball with Lillee in the Centenary Test at Lord's in 1980.

That legendary bowler and critic Bill O'Reilly had told Pascoe's father to remind his son he was not playing just for himself but for the ghosts of the past had only served to heighten Pascoe's nervousness. To a man the cricket community understood that O'Reilly did not mince words, and in the 1960s had famously and loudly told his down-and-out teammate 'Chuck' Fleetwood-Smith to never again sully the baggy green by wearing

Bill Brown at his Brisbane home with hats and caps in March 2007. (Newspix)

it when drinking with his hobo mates beneath the Princes Bridge in Melbourne. Pascoe said: 'Players recognise the sense of humility that comes with the cap and with wearing the cap.'

How Rodney Hogg, another forthright paceman of the period, would have enjoyed having Pascoe and company at his side, but the fair, green-eyed tearaway was pressed into service under Graham Yallop's leadership against England in 1978–79 at the height of the World Series Cricket upheaval and essentially had to fend for himself and carry the attack. 'I went into an Australian side so raw there was no one really to impart the traditions of the baggy green,' Hogg said. Hogg's Test career prospered for the next six years and earned him 123 wickets at 28.24 with two 10-wicket match hauls.

Marnus Labuschagne, shown here in 2021, had been presented his cap on debut three years earlier by Mike Hussey. 'His wise words still stick with me,' Labuschagne said. (Alamy)

These days there is not an elite player in the country who does not know the traditions of the baggy green. Given the chance, each will impart that legacy to those chosen to follow in their stead.

MC

Brett Lee with baggy green in the Lord's dressing room in 2005. (Newspix)

CHAPTER 2

The road to the baggy green

Australian captains, most notably Mark Taylor and Steve Waugh, have emphasised the significance and uniqueness of wearing the baggy green Australian cricket cap. Although this famous cap is now an integral part of the Australian cricket team's uniform, in the years before Federation in 1901 this was not the case. Before the formation of the Australian Cricket Council (1892–1900), Australian teams playing in England wore a variety of colours because no team uniform existed. The absence of a national cricket organisation in Australia ensured that this situation continued into the early years of Federation.

It wasn't until 1994 that a short paper, 'The Origin of the Green and Gold', published in the Australian Society for Sports History's journal *Sporting Traditions*, established that the 1899 Australians in England, captained by Joe Darling, were the first Australian cricket team to adopt these famous colours when they wore a green and gold cap replete with an Australian coat of arms. They also wore a matching gum-tree green blazer trimmed with wattle gold and with the coat of arms on the pocket over the heart.[5]

The distinguished historian Richard Cashman pointed out that in the 21st century the baggy green cap is a unique national icon that has achieved almost reverential status. 'It is one of the best-known brands in the country, enjoying a similar pre-eminent status in Australia to the All Black jersey in New Zealand ... The baggy green cap has been treated as an exclusive symbol that includes no sponsor logos and is not available for sale.'[6]

To examine how the cap evolved into its present colour and shape it is necessary to study the various colours and uniform designs worn by the Australian teams that visited Britain in the second half of the 19th century.

The first group of Australian cricketers to tour England was the Aboriginal team of 1868, which was managed by the former Surrey professional Charles Lawrence. This ground-breaking team apparently did not use a standard uniform or team colours. There is no image of the squad in a uniform, although a collage in the Marylebone Cricket Club collection at Lord's shows four of the players wearing a dark, long-sleeved shirt with a light sash or diagonal stripe across the front.[7] This collage also suggests that other players in the team wore a variety of Victorian club colours and caps or just personal cricket attire; however, a rare hand-coloured cabinet card produced during the lead-up games in Australia shows each player wearing a distinctly coloured cap.

The name of each player associated with each cap is listed at the bottom of the card, allowing ready identification. This was a portent for the future: today's Australian one-day cricketers, and more recently their opponents, have their names printed on the backs of their shirts. In 2019 Cricket Australia announced that from later in the year the Test shirt would carry the player's surname and number on the back. One of the tourists was officially known as 'Red Cap', suggesting that the practice of individually coloured caps for the Aboriginal cricketers was more prevalent than modern historians suppose.

The 1878 Australians wore a uniform of white and sky blue, the colours of the East Melbourne Cricket Club. Their blazers were white with sky-blue vertical stripes. The headwear was an unusual white cap with two horizontal sky-blue bands without a peak or brim. The cap was shaped like an inverted pudding bowl, a design that might have been borrowed from some English cricket teams such as I Zingari or the football teams of Eton and Harrow. An evocative oil painting in the Rex Nan Kivell Collection in the National Library of Australia depicting play during the

Charles Bannerman depicted wearing a striped cap in an image used for a rare 1878 cricket card. In reality the headwear was a pillbox shape, not a cap, and the stripes were horizontal, not vertical. (Image courtesy of Andrew Pickering)

tour's first match, against Willsher's Gentlemen at Chilham Castle in Kent, shows several Australians sporting the round, oddly shaped cap.[8]

Photographs and coloured lithographs of the 1878 tourists demonstrate clearly that there was no logo or coat of arms on their caps or blazers. This is confirmed by the well-known lithograph by 'Spy' of Fred Spofforth, Australia's opening bowler. This beautiful print clearly shows

Spofforth wearing his blue and white cap with matching tie and blazer, standing rather nonchalantly with his hands in his pockets. It was made available with copies of *Vanity Fair* published on 13 August 1878 and is now a rare collector's item.

This seminal tour was a private venture organised by John Conway, a former Melbourne Cricket Club (Melbourne CC) player. The tour was not sanctioned by the cricket associations of New South Wales or Victoria. Whether or not the East Melbourne club helped sponsor the tour is unclear, as no relevant minutes from the club survive. The use of the club's distinctive colours during the tour does suggest that the club might have contributed in some way.

The Australian tour of 1880 featured blazers with black and magenta vertical stripes. There was no distinctive pocket or coat of arms on the blazer, and the very few available photographs of the team show no team cap. Except for the occasional top hat the players are bare-headed, although they might have worn their club or state caps while fielding. On the way home this team visited North America for a series of matches. A black and white lithograph from an unidentified New York magazine shows individual head and shoulder portraits of the players. Four are wearing caps similar in design to that of the 1878 Australians except that two thick horizontal circles on the caps appear to be a dark colour, which suggests the caps might have been magenta and black. Importantly, the caps display no logo, badge or coat of arms. During this tour the first Test match played on English soil took place at The Oval.

According to Richard Cashman, the famous 1882 Australian team wore the red, black and yellow colours of the 96th Regiment.[9] They enjoyed a resounding victory at The Oval in the only Test played that summer. As Philip Derriman pointed out, this team might have also worn their Australian club blazers on tour.[10] A lithograph or hand-coloured print reproduced in David Frith's *Pageant of Cricket* depicts some of the players sporting a variety of coloured blazers. Spofforth, Harry Boyle and the captain Billy Murdoch wear emerald green blazers with thick, dark green vertical stripes,[11] while Tom Horan's blazer has dark brown vertical stripes. George Bonnor is the only player not in cricket attire: he wears a handsome brown suit. Six of the players wear identical dark green skullcaps, but there is no badge or coat of arms on either the blazers or the caps. This formal group portrait was most likely composed during or soon

During the Australian cricket tour of England in 1882 the team wore caps and blazers of red, black and yellow. (Alamy)

after The Oval Test, which suggests that the team might have discarded the colours of the 96th Regiment as the tour progressed in favour of the blazers and caps shown in this seemingly official lithograph.

However, if the picture is a hand-coloured print it must be viewed with some scepticism as it may have been coloured some years after the tour. While visiting the Welsh book town of Hay-on-Wye during the 1997 Ashes tour of England I noticed the proprietor of a print shop blithely using watercolours on an old black and white newspaper print of the 1886 Australians in England. He was painting their striped blazers in green and gold, which of course was incorrect because the 1886 team wore magenta, blue and white, the colours of the Melbourne Cricket Club. These old newspaper prints of Australian cricket teams in England can still be found today with incorrect team colours added years later.

The 1884 Australians in England wore caps and blazers of azure blue, identical in tint to the famous colours of the Italian national soccer side, the Azzurri. There are at least three items of evidence to support this assertion. The striking *Vanity Fair* lithograph by Carlo Pellegrini, known as 'Ape', of the giant Victorian batsman Bonnor shows him wearing the azure cap. Tantalisingly, the image is a side-on view and shows only a small portion of the badge on Bonnor's cap. The picture shows the part of the badge that is a gold circle enclosing what looks to be the tail of a kangaroo, also in gold, which suggests the presence of an Australian coat of arms on the cap.

Another piece of evidence is a beautiful hand-coloured Boyle and Scott lithograph in a private collection. Probably composed just after the tour, this lithograph shows the 1884 Australians in official pose wearing their azure blazers and caps. The Australian coat of arms is also featured but separately in a large circle underneath the image of the players. Close examination of the emblems on the caps and blazers suggests that the design on the cap might be of an emu and kangaroo holding a shield within a gold circle, as suggested by the Ape photogravure of Bonnor. The blazer pocket was decorated with a coat of arms without the enclosing circle. The shield within the coat of arms contains in clockwise direction the images of a sheep, sailing ship, sheaf of wheat and crossed miner's pick and shovel. These items were divided by a cross containing four of the stars of the Southern Cross. Above the shield was the symbol of the rising sun.

There is further evidence to suggest that the 1884 Australians may have been the first to wear an Australian coat of arms on their blazers, as the Boyle and Scott lithograph suggests. The Bradman Museum in Bowral has a royal blue blazer with a cricketer's coat of arms on the blazer. The kangaroo is on the right of the shield and the emu on the left, with the rising sun above the shield: the same order of the emu and kangaroo as in the Boyle and Scott lithograph. The blazer is thought to have belonged to Spofforth and was owned previously by the late CEO of the New South Wales Cricket Association Bob Radford, a devotee of cricket history. These three pieces of evidence strongly suggest that the 1884 Australians were the first team to wear a distinctly Australian coat of arms but were not the first to wear 'Advance Australia' on their uniform, as this important motto is not on the Spofforth blazer.

In 1886 the Australians in England donned the famous magenta, blue and white colours of their sponsor, the Melbourne CC. (Image courtesy of Michael Fahey)

In 2008 we advised that the 1886 Australians in England donned the famous magenta, blue and white colours of their sponsor, the Melbourne CC. The cap and blazer both displayed the well-known Melbourne CC emblem.[12] More recent research by the Australian Sports Museum uncovered information about the sixth Australian cricket team in England. *The Sydney Morning Herald* of 18 June 1888 on page 9 reported: 'McDonnell informed me that the men would play in the colours of the most famous of all Australian elevens – that of 1882 – red and yellow, with a thin strip of black. These colours were, I believe, adopted from the regiment of British foot at that time known as the 96th.' The 1888 Australians were also sponsored by the Melbourne CC and wore identical caps and blazers to those worn by their 1886 predecessors.

The 1890 Australians were photographed in England wearing dark blue blazers and caps, each with gold trim and an Australian coat of arms: a uniform that closely resembled that worn by the 1884 side. The motto 'Advance Australia', which was incorporated into this 1890 coat of arms, was very popular throughout the land as the push toward nationhood gathered momentum. Today's cricketers wear baggy green caps with only 'Australia' underneath the coat of arms. The 'Advance Australia' motto was in use on the Victorian goldfields as far back as 1853, the year before the Eureka Stockade uprising. An S.T. Gill painting from that year that depicts the decorations for a subscription ball, housed in the Art Gallery of Ballarat, shows the words 'Advance Australia' clearly printed in a scroll with a shield containing the Southern Cross, which was soon to become the symbol of the Eureka uprising.

The 1893 Australian cricket team, the eighth to tour England, adopted a striking emblem incorporating the four main stars of the Southern Cross within a curved shield. This design is similar to that shown in the S.T. Gill painting 40 years earlier. Each star was joined by a white Crusader-like cross; however, there was no use on the shield of either the kangaroo or emu or the motto 'Advance Australia'. This emblem was sewn onto the left blazer pocket and the players' skullcaps.[13]

At a meeting of the Australasian Cricket Council (later the Australian Cricket Board) in Adelaide on 8 January 1895, Percy Sheridan from New South Wales successfully proposed that the selection of colours for future Australian teams be decided by a subcommittee. Although the council was not a fundraising body, it was the governing body of cricket in Australia before the Board of Control was formed. Part of the council's charter was the 'regulation of visits of Australian teams to England and elsewhere'. The council also approved the appointment of national selectors. The council's meeting at the Oxford Hotel in Sydney on 8 October 1895 decided to send an Australian team to England in 1896.

No minutes exist to clarify what recommendations the council's subcommittee on the choice of the Australia XI's colours made, nor what influence any decision exerted on the 1896 players. However, the Special Correspondent for *The Sydney Morning Herald* filed this report from Colombo on 1 April 1896: 'Agreements for the tour were all signed when the Cuzco was about 10 miles out of Albany, and therefore within the jurisdiction of the British Courts, which extend 30 miles from British ports. The team now seems thoroughly satisfied and content that after all the best selection has been made . . . The night before Colombo, an important meeting of the team was held in the saloon. The selection committee was voted for, and the result was a little surprising. It consists

Ricky Ponting pensive in his baggy green after Australia's loss at Trent Bridge in 2005. (Newspix)

of Harry Trott (who was elected captain), George Giffen and Syd Gregory. The colours of the team were also decided upon, and are to be the same as those worn by the 1890 team – dark blue coats and caps with gold binding, the Australian arm on each article.'

During the Second Test match at the Melbourne Cricket Ground (MCG) in January 1898 the Australians wore the dark blue caps of the Victorian XI. At this time it was customary to wear the colours of the host state team. Mostyn Evan, the South Australian member of the Australasian Cricket Council's subcommittee on the cricket colours, is reported to have suggested 'a very attractive arrangement of green and gold colours' for the forthcoming 1899 tour of England.

The 10th Australian team to tour England obviously took note of Evan's suggestion, as they became the first Australian sports team to wear what became our national colours. Shortly after their arrival on the mail steamer *Ormuz* the Australians raised a green and gold flag at the Inns of Court Hotel in High Holborn, London, their headquarters for the summer.[14] *The Nepean Times* of 10 June 1899 informed its readers that 'A great amount of interest was manifested among members of the team when being measured for their blazers [the colours, by the by, are sage green and gold and green with gold-braided edge] as to who would have the greatest development. Howell was easily the first with 45 inches. Jones next with 42 inches.'

The decorative menu for the farewell dinner for the 1899 Australians at their London hotel is appropriately tied with deep green and bright gold ribbons, colours that would become synonymous with the emerging spirit of the new nation. From this time all Australian cricket teams touring England wore dark green blazers and caps with gold trimming, both decorated with the now-familiar kangaroo and emu–adorned coat of arms, which was almost identical to that worn by the 1884, 1890 and 1896 Australian sides. This design featured a sailing ship, slaughtered sheep, sheaf of wheat and miner's pick and shovel within four segments of a shield intersected by stars of the Southern Cross. However, the kangaroo was on the left of the shield and the emu on the right, as it is today. The motto 'Advance Australia' was included underneath in gold wire thread.

The green and gold striped blazers worn by the 1993–94 Australian XI were a first but were obviously influenced by Australian club cricketers in the early half of the 20th century. This team, however, wore the traditional baggy green cap, which was almost identical to that worn by Joe Darling's 1899 Australians in England almost 100 years previously.

It was not until after Federation that the green and gold colours of the Australian XI were first seen on home soil. The host team sported our national colours during the second Test against Archie MacLaren's Englishmen, which began at the MCG on 1 January 1902.[15] These colours were not ratified by the infant Board of Control until 1908. Meeting in Melbourne on 29 May, the board passed a motion that the official colours for future Australian cricket teams be 'Gum-tree Green and Gold'. This official sanction for a combination of colours that had been in use for nine years set the seal on the future use of the green and gold on Australian caps

Victor Trumper and his beloved 1899 cap. (Image courtesy of Michael Fahey)

and blazers for generations. The cap did not become baggy in appearance until after World War I, with players of Trumper's era wearing a tight-fitting green and gold cap.

The 1899 Australian touring side in England began the proud tradition of the green and gold cap and blazer with the cricket style coat of arms, as distinct from the official Australian coat of arms. Confirming cricket's standing as the national game, green and gold eventually became Australia's official national colours.

PS

Bert Oldfield in the nets at Lord's in England in 1930 in his Advance Australia baggy green. (Alamy)

CHAPTER 3

The gum-tree green and gold

In a world of instant gratification and increasingly meaningless accolades, the Australian Test cricket cap or baggy green is a mark of rare distinction, a national icon. A release in 2006 of a limited-edition lithograph by Legends Genuine Memorabilia[16] was titled 'The Pride of the Baggy Green'. This lithograph[17] was the genesis of the research that evolved into this book, because during the memorabilia project it became clear there had been little research into the cap's evolution and history.

The timeline of caps in the lithograph started with Victor Trumper and continued through to the game's greatest player Don Bradman and the cap he wore when he first captained Australia. The trilogy was completed with the cap of Steve Waugh, the baggy green's most public face. These caps are truly the highlight of this unique, unifying symbol, and they relate the fascinating story of the cap's evolution and represent both the history of the baggy green and Australian Test cricket.

The current cap can be traced back to the cap and colours adopted by the visionary members of the 1899 touring team to England, as discussed in Chapter 2. In one of cricket's serendipitous coincidences, the green cap with the Australian

43

cricket coat of arms made its Test debut in the first Test at Trent Bridge, Nottingham – as did Victor Trumper, the game's most stylish batsman and a great admirer of the Australian cap. His contemporary, Clem Hill, wrote that Trumper formed a strong attachment to the cap: 'It was bottle green, but nevertheless he stuck to it to the end and there was always no end of bother if [Reg] Duff or some of the other humorists of the side got hold of the cap and hid it.'[18]

Clem Hill and wicketkeeper J.J. Kelly on tour in 1905 in Australian skullcaps. (Alamy)

The colours adopted by the members of this team before the Tests, green and gold, became the colours for all Australian sporting teams. While the game's administrators did not officially adopt the gum-tree green and gold colours and coat of arms until 1908, these 1899 colours and design were different from and predated the current Australian Commonwealth coat of arms, which was adopted in 1912. The cricket coat of arms is one of the few pre-Federation symbols in use today.

The official Australian livery colours were blue and gold until 1984, when the Hawke government adopted green and gold as the national colours. The decision of the 1899 team to incorporate these colours with the coat of arms was a defining moment in Australian sport, as the colours were adopted by the Australian Olympic team in 1908, the Australian rugby league Kangaroos in 1928 and rugby union's Wallabies the year after.

The long ancestry of the baggy green and the continuity in its design mean there is a strong sense of legacy and obligation for those selected as an Australian Test cricketer. Allan Border, a driving force behind the first reunion of Australian Test cricketers held in Sydney in 2000, revealed his inspiration: 'In Australian cricket, one of our strengths has always been a good team spirit. Don Bradman played in a baggy green, so did Victor Trumper and all the blokes over the years. So there's a realisation when you get given that cap you're part of something special.'[19]

Jack Gregory (back row, second from left) wearing his old skullcap, while teammates in the 1921 touring side to England have adopted the newer baggy style still worn today. (Image courtesy of Ronald Cardwell)

The baggy green has a uniquely Australian feel. Originally, it was a skullcap, like those commonly worn in England. From 1920, however, the cap had a 'baggy' or Australian style; generally this word is applied to all Test caps from 1899. The distribution of the Test and state caps reflects the egalitarian nature of Australian society. Every player receives a cap on selection, whereas in England caps are awarded to denote status and seniority. A player could remain uncapped even after years of representing his country.[20]

This sense that Australian values, history and legacy are represented in the cap re-emerged in the 1990s. In November 1994 Mark Taylor instituted the practice of the whole team wearing the cap during the first fielding session of each Test match.[21] Steve Waugh said he had suggested this initiative in a team meeting. In any case, Waugh heightened the public perception of the players' respect for the cap when he wore his baggy green until it almost fell apart. He ignored calls to replace the cap, although he did bow to pressure and had the peak repaired by Albion in 2002. Waugh received more than one baggy green cap during his career and certainly wore more than one cap, but a single one was worn for the vast majority of his career: the cap that was repaired.

Now each Test player is handed his baggy green by a former player in a ceremony on the morning of his first Test. 'It is such a special time for a player and the old procedure certainly lacked polish,' Taylor said.[22] The formal ceremony instituted by Taylor in 1996 was refined by Waugh, who thought a former Australian Test player should do the presentation. This practice has been copied by rugby union's Wallabies and South Africa's Springboks.

In an age when professional sports are inextricably linked to sponsorship, the baggy green and team blazer stand alone in their purity. Cricket Australia (CA) has steadfastly refused to commercialise the cap by putting sponsors' logos on it and it has never offered replicas for sale, thereby ensuring that no imitation can sully this most prestigious of prizes. Steve Waugh reinforced this when discussing his cap's repair: 'It gives me power and the team aura. It's something people recognise and respect and, most importantly, it has never been commercialised in any way, nor does it have sponsor logos on it.'[23]

A small replica cap was specially produced for former players and presented to them at the 2003 reunion. The plan was for these caps to uniquely bear that player's Test number embroidered on the back, but logistical complexities prevented that from occurring. However, a plaque at presentation listed each player's Test number. Former Test captain Bill Brown, a member of the 1948 Invincibles and at the time Australia's oldest Test player, expressed his pleasure in receiving a new cap, as he had not kept any old ones. 'I don't know what happened. I probably gave them away. We valued the caps when we received them, but they seem to have become more special in recent times.'[24]

Receiving a baggy green is recognition of your acceptance into the highest level of Australian cricket, a cause for much celebration and congratulations, yet it is also a time for reflection as the cap is a reminder of all those who have gone before. The victories and losses, euphoria and heartache are all interlaced in the very fibres of that flannel halo, ensuring that all who wear it are entrusted with a legacy and responsibility of lasting national importance.

In 2003, then oldest living former Test player Bill Brown (90) posed with then Test captain Steve Waugh when 147 past and present Australian Test cricketers gathered for a presentation reunion. (Newspix)

To many, Steve Waugh personifies the cap and the importance of its legacy: 'The ultimate goal is to wear the Baggy Green cap. There's something special about putting that cap on – for me anyway. There's no way you will catch me wearing a white hat. The cap's always on my head. There's an aura about the Australian cap.'[25]

As with any symbol the baggy green's meaning is personal, and for some it carries similar themes but with different emphasis to Waugh's. To Ian Chappell the message behind the symbolism of the cap is most important. In his foreword to *The Baggy Green* (New Holland Publishers, 1998) Chappell stated: 'The baggy green, Australian's cricket cap, is more a testimony to the characters who have worn it than a symbol of prestige . . . Nevertheless, in recent times the baggy green has gained in status.'

Chappell suggested the prices paid for Trumper caps at auction and the searches for a Bradman cap had elevated its status, and this was further reinforced by the pre-Test capping ceremony. While acknowledging these new traditions he contended: 'I'm sure that even the players who have grown up under this tradition will still remember the characters they played with long after they've forgotten where they stored their baggy green.' The players of previous eras certainly respected the cap and the club it signified but, as Chappell acknowledged, the emphasis changed dramatically in the few years up to 1998.

The baggy green of the new millennium is instantly recognisable as that worn throughout most of the 20th century. There have been some changes over the years but generally these have been short lived, although a few changes have been more enduring. The 1899 cap and the modern cap bear some differences, hence the introduction of the century-old replica lookalike in 2000 as an intentional and dramatic point of difference.

The current cap is made by Kookaburra Sport in Perth, whose association with the cap commenced at the New Year's Test in 2017. An announcement stated: 'CA regularly reviews its supplier contracts, and its minimum criteria for the Baggy Green were that the company be Australian owned, the caps be made of 100% Australian wool, and the manufacturing be done in Australia.'

For the 50 years until December 2016 the cap had been handcrafted exclusively under official licence by Albion Hat and Cap Company Pty Ltd. It was 100 per cent Australian wool and was officially described as 'bottle green woollen flannel'. Early manufacturers were Potts and Wilkinson in

In Fred Spofforth's day, circa 1878, Australian cricketers wore blue and white-striped caps and blazers.

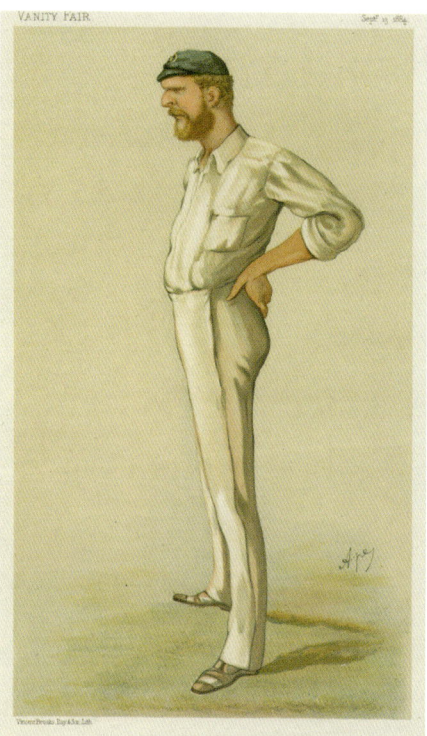

By 1884 Australian cricketers such as George John Bonner sported blue caps and blazers, the latter with a coat of arms.

Victor Trumper's baggy green for the tour to England in 1909. Note the date below 'Advance Australia'. (Image courtesy of MCC Museum Lord's)

Edgar Mayne (left) and his cap for the triangular series with South Africa and England in 1912. (Images courtesy of Alamy and National Library of Australia)

A bronze sculpture of a 1926 baggy green, a tribute to Charlie Macartney, was installed at the Prince Henry Hospital site at Little Bay on Macartney Oval. (Images courtesy of sculptor Anika Asplund, Teknemodus Pty Ltd)

Colour drawing of Charlie Macartney in cap by Arthur Mailey from 1927. (Image courtesy of James Merchant)

Don Bradman with the cap worn for the home series with South Africa in 1931-32. For that series only, two dates adorned the cap.

Bradman's cap for the 1936-37 Ashes series. Dates appeared on the caps from 1930-31 to 1972. (Image courtesy of Legends Genuine Memorabilia)

A rare image of Bradman in colour wearing his famous 1948 cap. This image was taken at Lord's two days before the second Test. (Alamy)

Keith Miller's cap from the 1949–50 tour of South Africa.

Richie Benaud poses in his baggy green at Lord's during the 1961 Ashes series. (Alamy)

Johnny Martin's 1963–64 cap is adorned with the Commonwealth coat of arms. It appeared on the cap for just one series. (Image courtesy of Michael Fahey)

Lots of bare heads among the 1972 Australians in England at Lord's, Keith Stackpole and Ian Chappell leading the way. (Alamy)

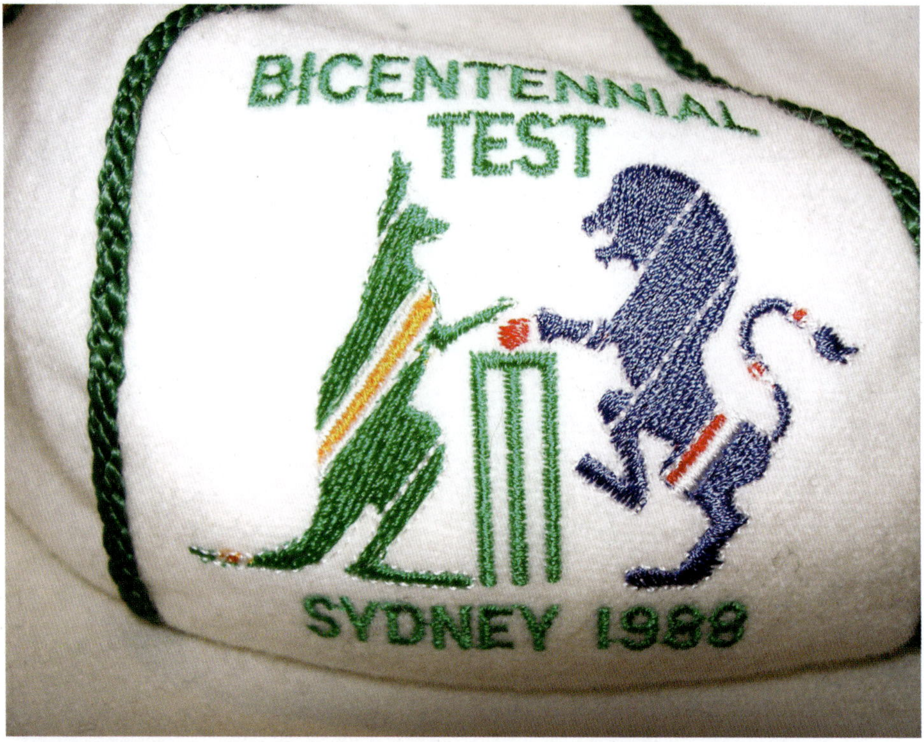

The 1988 Bicentennial Test cap (white) not worn but awarded to both the England and Australia teams. The 2000 Millennium cap (below left) and the 2001 Centenary of Federation baggy green. (Image courtesy of Craig Hawkins)

1899, Rowan Glasgow in 1921, Harding's Mercery in 1924 to 1925 and 1928 to 1929 and Scholium, who made a version of the 1930 touring cap. It appears that some touring caps were made in Britain until a long-term supplier was found. The Farmer's Sydney label appeared on the cap from 1931 to 1932, then until the early 1970s the label reflected that the licence and production had been entrusted to Albion. It appears Albion had produced the cap for Farmer's since the 1950s.

The minutes of cricket's administrative body since 1899 contain scant mentions of the cap's manufacturer.[26] At the board meeting of 30–31 December 1931 and 1 January 1932 it was recorded that 'a tender for production of caps and blazers was accepted from Farmer's. Farmer's had offered to do the job for 5 pounds 10 shillings and sixpence, beating other tenderers David Jones and Hardings.' Another mention from the board meeting of September 1946 noted that the 'cost of Farmer's services was disaggregated as follows: blazers 2 pounds 19 shillings and sixpence, pocket badge 1 pound 5 shillings, caps 11 shillings and sixpence'. These notes are purely administrative confirmations, with no hint that the cap was anything more than just another piece of apparel such as sweaters or boots.

The label of Farmer's department store appeared inside the cap for 40 years from 1931 to 1932. This example was Keith Miller's. (Image Michael Fahey)

Albion continued to use the original patterns and wooden blocks to cut the panels for their five standard sizes, and there is provision for players to have a cap custom made to ensure a perfect fit. Commencing in the mid-1990s, there was a continuing dialogue between Albion and the players. Caps were adjusted once they had been worn for a period of time, and Albion steam cleaned and repaired any caps worn for 100 or more Tests. This process ensured that the caps remained comfortable and presentable.

The cap's essential elements are its shape, cloth, the components of the coat of arms – shield, scroll and crest – and any use of dates. All of these have changed at times over the years, and although presented as a constant the baggy green has in fact been a continuing work.

Victor Trumper's 1899 cap could more correctly be termed a skullcap.

With the cricket board's minutes silent as to the changes over the years, it can be assumed that these occurred for a variety of pragmatic reasons often made by administrators or the manufacturers. Before computerised embroidery machines the sewing was done by hand, therefore design variations — for example, in the shape and size of the kangaroo and emu on the coat of arms — occurred depending on the person embroidering them. Changes in the company manufacturing the cap in the 1920s and 1930s also produced variations.

From 1899 the shape of the cap evolved from skull to baggy and the material from velvet to woollen flannel. Why and when did the Test cap become baggy? It would appear that no conscious decision was made, that subtle shifts occurred based upon prevailing fashion.

The design of headwear varied greatly in the latter part of the 19th century: there were top hats, pill boxes, pudding tops and skullcaps, a variety that was reflected on the cricket field. The first Test caps in 1878 contained no peak, and tight skullcaps were in vogue from 1890 until the 1909 Ashes tour. The 1912 cap appears to be somewhat fuller but not yet fully baggy. With the cessation of tours during World War I, the next Test series for Australia was not until 1920. In this home series the Australians all wore a baggy-style cap, and strictly this was when the baggy green was born.

Supporting the theory that fashion had a role in the evolution, the photographs taken by the player–manager of the 1905 tourists Frank Laver[27] show the playing cap as being very tight. However, interspersed with these photos are images of the same players in daywear sporting fuller-styled caps. Clearly this style was favoured by the players away from the field.

Given the intensity of the Australian sun compared to England's, a larger cap with a peak that provided some shade for the face would be favoured by cricketers. The adoption of a home-grown design also showed a growing confidence in being distinctly Australian and not slavishly adopting all the trends of the mother country. The baggy style was quickly identified with Australians, in stark contrast to the multitude of caps worn by Englishmen.

An article on the great Australian batsman Charlie Macartney by D.J. Knight, published in *Country Life* on 17 June 1926, stated:

> *Lastly, surmounting all – the cap. There are many cricketers that one cannot truly picture in the mind's eye without the headgear which seems inseparable from, and without which they would no longer seem to retain their personality. Plum Warner at Lord's without his harlequin cap (like Jacob's coat of many colours) is unthinkable – it is no longer 'Plum', but some stranger, unrecognisable, unfamiliar almost unfriendly. Macartney is no exception – the little eager bird-like figure, not unlike a perky cock sparrow, is completed and adorned with the queer [sic] cap of his country, which seems always too large for him, and whose peak, shaped like a jockey's, seems to dominate and envelope the whole of his figure.*[28]

The baggy shape is achieved in the final stages of manufacture. Beginning its life as eight panels and a peak, the cap is sewn together, sized, blocked and finally tacked, which involves pulling the cap over the peak and sewing it down with four stitches. This gives it the unique baggy appearance. During the 1997 Ashes series there were suggestions that the cap's shape was changing.[29] Albion and the Australian team manager Alan Crompton confirmed that the caps were being made the same way with the same block and patterns.

Two years later[30] Glenn McGrath was identified as the culprit who had lifted the crown and inadvertently detached the stitches, which highlighted the vigilant nature of those watching to ensure that the cap remained the same. The issue that evokes passion is the fact that the cap has not changed since the 1930s and that it is a 'symbolic torch that one generation of Australian players passes on to the next. It is its unchangeability that sets it apart.'[31]

Judging by the caps still in existence, the 1899 version was the only one produced in velvet. Subsequent caps, namely from 1907 and 1909, are made of a woven cotton material. Discussion with Albion, the manufacturer of the 2000 skullcap, revealed that embroidering onto velvet is a difficult operation[32] and it is possible these difficulties precluded velvet's continued use. Cost may also have been a factor. The 1930 Scholium-manufactured cap had two metal punch holes on either side, presumably for ventilation. This is the only cap with this feature.

Even in the 21st century, the cap's third century, the players continue to help mould the cap and its appearance. Traditionally, Albion lined the cap with its generic inner label, a circular cloth patch bearing the words 'Albion, C&D, official suppliers to South African Cricket Union, New Zealand Cricket, Australian Cricket Board'. Albion learned that Justin Langer had blotted out the references on his cap's label to South Africa and New Zealand. In 2002 Albion redesigned the label and the baggy green now proudly states 'Official Australian Test cap'. Albion then took the specialisation a step further and designed the label in such a way that the players' Test numbers could be heat sealed onto the interior.[33] This change was not embraced, as tour managers needed to take several spare caps of varying sizes to ensure there was a good fit for any debutants. Again, pragmatism affected the cap's appearance.

The components of the baggy's coat of arms have also evolved. The scroll set below the shield and originally blue featured the words 'Advance Australia'. The colour changed to red soon after, and then in the early 1930s 'Advance' was dropped. Richard Cashman suggested this was done following a directive from the Commonwealth government,[34] which seems possible as the original 1908 Australian coat of arms did contain 'Advance Australia' but the 1912 – the current version – used 'Australia' only.

Similar coats of arms were used by sports, towns and cities from the 1850s and reflected important elements of Australian life and history: commerce, immigration, the production of sheep and wheat and the minerals extracted from the ground, represented by the picks. These elements of the shield are set around a Southern Cross and were supported by the uniquely Australian kangaroo and emu, set below the crest – a rising sun indicating a new dawn – and above the inspiring 'Advance Australia', which reflects the aspirations of the emerging nation.

The order of the four symbols was altered soon after 1899. On that cap the colours behind the symbols were blue, white, red and white clockwise from top left, as on the current cap, but the order of the symbols embroidered were first a ship, sheep, wheat and pick. Since 1909 at least the sheep and ship symbols have been reversed. Initially, the cross containing the white Southern Cross stars was gold, but since 1909 it has been embroidered in blue.

Warren Bardsley (left) and Edgar Mayne walk out to bat at Lord's during the Triangular Tournament Test against South Africa. Both wear the rare cap with the short-lived 1908 coat of arms. (Alamy)

It appears the cap carried a different coat of arms from the 1910–11 home Test series against South Africa to the 1912 triangular series in England. Photographs of these teams and a 1912 Edgar Mayne cap held by the National Museum of Australia show that the shield was white with a red cross enclosed. A kangaroo and emu support the shield with a star on top. This design was the first official coat of arms for the newly federated Australia and was granted by Edward VII in a royal warrant on 7 May 1908. Below the shield was 'Advance Australia'.

It's possible that it was adopted so the cap would match the official coat of arms. There is no mention of this in the board minutes, but one theory about the change is that the newly formed Board of Control was exerting its authority over the players. From 1905 to 1912 there were continual disputes between the Test players and the new board. One example of the friction concerned the 1909 tour to Britain. As Gideon Haigh noted: 'Even the team's notepaper caused irritation: [team manager William] McElhone insisted it bear the board's letterhead alongside the Australian XI symbol, which Laver griped would "spoil the looks of the neat and pretty heading".'[35]

Clearly the players, who previously toured as entrepreneurs sharing in the tour profits, resented the board's attempt to take control, but this dispute also shows that the players felt the Australia XI symbol – the coat of arms on the cap – was their symbol, not the board's. The fact that the players had created the emblem would have reinforced this sense of ownership. The cap may well have been a symbolic battlefield between two sides keen to establish their legitimacy: at the time, people often asked whether the players were representing the board or the nation. This series of disputes culminated in Victor Trumper, Warwick Armstrong, Vernon Ransford, Albert Cotter and Hanson Carter, called the 'big six' because of their high standing and reputations in Australian cricket, refusing to accept the board's conditions for touring Britain in 1912.

The official Australian coat of arms of 1908 made no reference to the states and several alterations were suggested, which resulted in the current Commonwealth coat of arms that was proclaimed, again by royal warrant, by George V on 19 September 1912. Significantly, this had just 'Australia' in the wreath. We have no explanation for why the 1908 arms was used by the cricket board for the cap after 1910, or why the board reverted to the original 1899 cricket coat of arms after World War I. It remains a mystery why the official coat of arms of 1912 was not adopted by cricket, as it was by other sports.

The shape of the shield has also varied. Generally, it has been presented as it is today: wider at the top and bottom with a narrow waist. In 1928–29 and again in 1930 the shield was even wider at the top and tapered to a point at the bottom. Similarly, the shape and size of the rising sun, kangaroo and emu have changed. The basic design of the shield supported by the kangaroo and emu was in use from at least 1884. The 1893 Australian team sported a shield on the cap and blazer, and the 1896 side included a kangaroo and emu. The original and current coat of arms has the kangaroo on the left and the emu on the right, but this positioning was reversed for the 1905, 1907–08 and 1909 teams.

Originally, the coat of arms was made with what is known as bullion embroidery, coloured metallic wire and silk thread. This is shown in intricate detail on the Trumper and Bradman caps as they were used up to 1938, the last tour before World War II. From 1946–47 to the current day the embroidery is comprised solely of cotton thread, though auction houses erroneously describe this as 'silk thread'.

There was one season when the Australian cap carried a different coat of arms. The 1963–64 cap sported the official Australian coat of arms as set out in the 1912 Royal warrant. The cap for the 1963–64 series against South Africa carried the kangaroo, emu and 'Australia' ribbon and sported the Commonwealth shield, which contains the individual crests of the six states and not the ship, sheep and so on. The rising sun was replaced by a six-pointed star, although the Commonwealth star has seven points. This crest, which sat on top of a blue and gold wreath, was featured on the blazer as well and appears to have been used only for that season. There is no official explanation for this, although one theory is that the coat of arms was replaced in response to the controversy over that summer's tour by the Springboks.

South Africa had just been expelled from the Imperial Cricket Conference (ICC) due to its apartheid policy and there was some dispute about the Test status of the series. A decision may have been taken to change the emblems to signify that the XI were representing Australia and not the Australian Board of Control. In an article in *The Australian* dated 7 February 2016 Gideon Haigh adds more to this theory. In October 1960 South Africa voted to leave the Commonwealth by becoming a republic,

Former Australian Test cricketer turned commentator Kerry O'Keeffe at home with dog Steve and his presentation miniature baggy green. (Newspix)

and under Rule 5 of the constitution of the Imperial Cricket Conference they were required to leave. This cost their matches Test status. The ICC at their meeting on 20 July 1961 was obliged to agree that Tests involving South Africa would become unofficial.

From 1930 to 1972 the date of each series was embroidered on the cap in the traditional place: below the scroll. There have been some exceptions to this: in 1909 the date was woven into the ribbon in the middle of 'Advance' and 'Australia'; in 1931–32, as modelled in a classic photo of Bradman, the date appeared on either side of the newly singular 'Australia'. There is no cap or image from 1930–31, but as the Farmer's tender was accepted during the New Year's Test in 1931–32 it seems that this was the first year of Farmer's manufacture and the board was merely ratifying what the administration had enacted. This may explain the new design with the dates either side of 'Australia'. What is known is that from 1932–33 to 1972 the cap's design remained the same, barring the 1963–64 cap. The current cap retains this design, with the lack of date and cotton thread the only changes from the Bodyline days.

Traditionally, players received numerous caps, especially when they were dated. A new cap was awarded for each series, and on some tours – notably the 1948 tour – players received two caps. This fact has only recently been uncovered; the accepted wisdom had been that one cap was issued for each series. The State Library of South Australia inquired into the issuing of caps when they were offered a second Bradman 1948 cap in 2004. The library's Bradman website states that 'The library approached Bradman's 1948 Invincibles teammates, Sam Loxton and Ron Hamence. Both clearly recalled receiving two caps for the tour in question. Also contacted was Barry Jarman, who kept wicket for Australia in the 1960s. He similarly recalled receiving two caps for each of the 1961, 1964, and 1968 tours of England.'

The issuing of two caps on the 1948 tour became irrefutable when, in July 2004, Barry Gibbs uncovered the existence of an original players' contract for that tour. He obtained a copy of the contract and found that paragraph 32 stated: 'The Board shall provide each player with a blazer, two caps, sweater and tie.'[36]

In the 1970s and 1980s the awarding of caps was not done automatically each season, although players from that era received several caps during their career. Albion's former managing director Tony Henson said that repeated requests for replacement caps by two senior players in the early 1980s alerted him to the possibility that the demand by the public for caps was becoming excessive. At his request the board set down rules for the allocation of baggy greens.[37] Since the 1990s the current policy, which is strictly enforced, stipulates that a player is presented with a cap on debut and that this will be his sole cap unless it is stolen or lost or if it needs to be replaced due to excessive wear.

In July 2007 Cricket Australia's kit manager, Adam Fraser, provided a copy of this policy: 'The baggy green is obviously presented to each player on the ground before the commencement of the first Test they're selected to play in. CA policy is that the baggy green shall not be replaced unless stolen or severely damaged. Players are required to fill in a form that verifies that their baggy has been lost, stolen, or damaged before consideration is given to issuing a new one. Generally, we find that players are very protective of their baggy greens and don't like to have them replaced.'

Now the awarding of a cap has evolved into a ceremony whereby a past player makes the presentation to the debutant, again reinforcing the legacy of the elite club of Australia Test cricketers. When the first edition of this book was written in 2008 this elite club had only 399 members, with Western Australia's Chris Rogers being Australian Test player No. 399. In 2023 there were 466 numbered Test players, with Matthew Kuhnemann debuting in that year. In a further mark of respect for the cap, Albion C&D made and presented to each player a bag to house the cap, further protecting it. Embroidered upon the bag was the player's name and Test number.

By 2008 three variations of the baggy green, ceremonial but match versions, had been made, and by 2023 this had increased. In the 1988 Bicentennial Test against England in Sydney the Australians were presented with a white baggy cap with green piping. This cap had a unique Bicentennial-inspired logo with a lion and kangaroo facing each other over a wicket. The English players were also presented with a baggy white as a souvenir. It should be noted that the Australians were presented with but didn't wear this cap in the match.

The resurgence of interest in the cap and its history resulted in replica commemorative caps being designed for the Sydney New Year's Day Tests of 2000 and 2001. These caps paid homage to previous designs; the first was a replica of the 1900 velvet skullcap.[38] 'This is the first Test of the new millennium and we thought we'd do something to celebrate playing for Australia,' Steve Waugh said. 'A couple of weeks ago I thought: "The first Test of the new millennium, what can we do to celebrate the fact we are playing for Australia?" It's a skullcap and it's a little bit different to the cap we wear now. It seems to give the players more character straightaway. You have got to know where you have come from to know where you are going. I think that's important in sport.'[39]

The 2000 velvet cap made by Albion used a lurex thread that gave it a slightly metallic sheen. It was a direct copy of the 1899 Trumper cap auctioned by Christies Australia in 1997. The 2001 commemorative cap with yellow piping celebrated the Centenary of Australia's Federation on 1 January 1901. While this design was depicted on cigarette cards of the Australian team issued in 1905,[40] it appears to be poetic licence as records suggest this style was never worn by an Australian Test team. The embroidery below the coat of arms on the 2001 commemorative says: 'Centenary of Federation Test Match 2001'.

Another variation was made for the inaugural ICC Super Series in October 2005 when the Australians, as the world's highest ranked team,

Steve Waugh and his weathered baggy green after his side defeated England at the Oval and retained the Ashes after a 4-1 series win in 2001. (Alamy)

played the World XI in a One Day International (ODI) and a Test match. While the normal design, the cap had the details of the series embroidered on its back panel: 'ICC Super Series Australia v World XI'.

A more recent addition, a commemorative centurion cap produced to acknowledge a player's 100th Test appearance, was first stuck for Michael Clarke's century in 2013. Players who had previously achieved that were presented with their cap as well. Embroidered on one side was '100th test' and the date of the match, and on the other side was the player's name and the word 'Centurion'.

Many assume the baggy pink made for the McGrath Foundation Pink Day on day three of every Sydney Test is a version of the Test cap. For the Australian teams it is not, as it carries the McGrath Foundation logo. The Australian team are photographed wearing them before the game and the caps are auctioned each year, but they don't have any Australian insignia on them. The fundraising theme was also adopted at Lords, and the Ruth Strauss Foundation celebrated its fifth year in 2023 with a Red Day at Lord's. In 2019 the Australian team wore a baggy red prior to the game, and this time they bore the CA logo (as worn on the non-Test caps) and all the Test and limited over gear (except for the baggy green).

State associations and museums received presentation copies of both the 2000 and 2001 caps, which was a generous and far-sighted initiative by the Australian Cricket Board (ACB) as the Western Australian Cricket Association, for instance, had no caps in its collection. The two donated formed the basis of a collection that then acquired the baggy green belonging to Western Australian Keith Slater, who played one Test against England in 1958–59.

Two other Test caps were produced, but only as prototypes that were not approved by the ACB. The first was submitted by Albion to the ACB to commemorate the first Test between Australia and Bangladesh, which was played in Darwin in July 2003. It was made from the candy-stripe material used in the blazers in the late 1990s. The second, made for the ICC Test match played in Sydney in October 2005, was a green cap with Petersham ribbon in concentric circles around the cap. There may well be a halt to dramatically different caps for a while.

Behind the scenes the ACB and then CA have grappled with the problem of protecting its trademarks, images and intellectual property from unauthorised use. In the late 1990s Coopers Brewing Company produced a marketing poster in which baggy green caps were portrayed as bottle tops on pictures of bottled beer.[41] Entitled 'Coopers salutes some of Australia's most famous green caps', it listed all the post-war Test captains' names under a cap. The board had not approved this use of its intellectual property and received no royalty from the promotion. More importantly, the use of the caps to promote a product cut across existing sponsorship deals and was a significant threat to a legitimate sponsor's rights. Legal advice given to the board indicated it had little recourse because trademark protection was not available: coats of arms were prohibited marks. CA then registered a distinct brand it could use for all its uniforms, memorabilia and merchandise. Eventually, legal protection was granted to CA for its coat of arms and the term 'baggy green'.

In 2002–03 the ACB rebranded itself as Cricket Australia and a new logo was created. The board's annual report said: 'The new brand mark incorporates the kangaroo and emu from the traditional cricket coat of arms, the Southern Cross, Australia's green and gold colours and a sunburst, representing the traditional relationship between cricket and the Australian summer.' Importantly, 'the cherished baggy green cap has not changed. After consultation with players and other stakeholders about a suitable approach for Australia's most famous cap, it was agreed that the iconic baggy green should remain in its current form. It will keep the traditional cricket coat of arms emblem.'[42]

The traditional coat of arms was retained on the baggy green and helmet. The new CA logo is now used on the Test and ODI shirts, Test jumpers and the ODI cap. Tradition had partially defeated a considerable commercial problem. Supported by the players, the cap, in conjunction with the coat of arms, was too powerful a symbol to be discarded, but the coat of arms was removed from shirts, sunhats and jumpers due to market pressures.

While the legal question regarding the protection of trademarks and brands was resolved, there were still commercial reasons to reinvent the logo. Part of the reasoning was that the cricket associations of the states would adopt the design and base their logos on it, thus the new CA tagline 'The Backyard to the Baggy Green' could then be seen on all cricket branding. A quick look at each state association's website, however, shows that the Northern Territory is the only state or territory to adopt CA's template. Despite the merits of the plan, the other associations chose to retain the benefits that had already accrued from their own logos.

Australia's rigid non-commercialisation of the Test cap is at odds with the traditions of other countries. In England, players such as Plum Warner, Douglas Jardine and Percy Chapman played Test cricket in a club or college cap. In 1971 A.J.M. Hewitt wrote: 'Always there was a remarkable display of coloured caps at country house cricket and the identity of the amateurs, who appeared intermittently in first-class cricket, could as a rule be deduced from the caps or sweaters they sported. These caps might, on occasions, become dramatically symbolic as, for instance, the harlequin cap of D.R. Jardine that so provoked the Sydney "Hillites".'[43]

As recently as 1996 the English county Surrey still had a system where the awarding of a cap created a professional elite. The former Australian fast bowler and erstwhile Cricket New South Wales chief executive David Gilbert found that when he arrived at The Oval in 1996, capped and uncapped players changed on either side of the Surrey wall: a partition that dominated the dressing room.[44] Gilbert had the wall removed. The England team in the 1990s took to the field in a variety of caps, some faded, some baseball style. This was understandable given the amateur/professional dichotomy of English cricket and the resulting dress conventions, and also the fact that the England touring cap was different from the one worn at home. Tours used to be undertaken as the Marylebone Cricket Club until the 1960s and the touring cap was blue with a St George and dragon emblem, while the home cap sported three lions under a crown.

In Karachi in September 1988 Pakistan's Javed Miandad scored a double century against Australia. After commencing in a helmet, he found it uncomfortable in the heat and swapped to a cap. What perplexed the Australians who had grown up with the tradition of the baggy green cap was that Miandad's cap boasted the words 'I love New York'. Sadly, the grainy footage of the Test now online does not show the cap clearly.

Indian cricket could also learn from the Australian attitude to its cap and traditions. In 2000 Sunil Gavaskar bemoaned the variety of caps worn and the haphazard respect for the cap and the Indian logo. 'There are many lessons the Indian team can learn from this tour. One of them is the respect for tradition . . . The Indians should take a leaf out of their opponent's book on matters like Australia's adoption of the 1900-style cap for the final Test.'[45]

Australian captain Pat Cummins at Headingley in 2023 with his well-worn baggy green. (Alamy)

Gavaskar was upset that a specially designed player-only cap was given to members of the media covering the tour. He believed a 3–0 defeat by Australia came as no surprise when pride in playing for your country was so diminished. The Indians wore three types of caps: the standard type and others with the players' names embroidered on them, while vice-captain Sourav Ganguly's cap carried advertising as well as his name.

An interesting article by journalist Rohit Brijnath appeared in *Sportstar* magazine in 2001. Comparing Australia and India and the traditions of the two cricket teams, he wrote: 'Paradoxically, Australia, a land of unending sameness, culturally not so much impoverished as similar, worships tradition and finds great strength in ritual when it comes to sport.'

Brijnath then set out the various Australian cricket rituals: the cap presentation, the singing by the players of 'Under the Southern Cross' after every Test win, bowlers holding the ball up after five-wicket hauls and the Test numbers on the shirts. He quoted Gavaskar from the story above and suggested: 'Not everything demands imitation . . . but to dismiss Australia's rituals as foreign, thus useless (as we tend to) is an act of ignorance. Any ritual that binds a team together into a purposeful, proud unit is worth embracing. Any custom that links India's cricketing generations is worth starting.'[46]

As a point of difference, Nasser Hussain noted in his autobiography *Playing with Fire* (Penguin, 2005): 'Waugh could overdo the love of the baggy green cap. He wore it to Wimbledon to support Australian tennis players and I felt it was a bit of a "look at me" sort of thing. I hated it when an Australian would tell you they cared more or had a mental edge over us.' He suggested that he and most other players of his era also cared deeply about playing for their country (in this case England), and rather tellingly he suggested that Australia had the 'edge' as they were just purely and simply a better team.

While these are understandable sentiments, it should be noted that the recognition of the baggy green's traditions, including its wearing and presentation, was devised to produce a better team. The Australians might have played better, but undoubtedly the cap and its new traditions contributed to this performance.

The final word comes from Steve Waugh, the man who personified the Australian cap in this period and intertwined traditions with the demands of the present: 'The ultimate goal is to wear the baggy green cap. There's something special about putting that cap on – for me anyway. There's no way you will catch me wearing a white hat. The cap's always on my head. There's an aura about the Australian cap.'[47]

MF

Part of the Jason Brooks collection.
(Image courtesy of Michael Fahey)

CHAPTER 4

Collectors

The word 'cricketania' was first used in London society in August 1862, when it related to 'literature, sayings or gossip' about cricket.[48] In the *Cricketer Winter Annual* 1921–22, F.S. Ashley-Cooper wrote that the 'collection of "cricketania" has again come in vogue'. The Cricketania Society was founded in October 1929 with the aim of creating a register of collectors and collating a census of rare publications and cricketania. It folded in 1935 and no similar body existed in Britain until the formation of the Cricket Memorabilia Society in 1987.

In the preface to *The Wisden Book of Cricket Memorabilia*, the authors acknowledge that collecting was 'an arcane pursuit, dominated by a handful of collectors and part-time dealers, but the advent of regular sales by leading London auction houses in 1978 has brought it to a far wider audience and attracted a far wider range of materials on to the market.'[49]

The Marylebone Cricket Club (Marylebone CC) bicentenary auction of 1987 realised £320,000, and it is estimated that other auctions in the previous decade had collectively realised only £680,000. Overall, some 11,000 lots had sold for an average of about £90 each. If 1978 saw the birth of serious collecting, then the Marylebone CC auction of 1987 took it to another level in terms of prices achieved.

Currently there are at least a dozen auction companies dealing in cricket memorabilia worldwide, and scores of dealers who primarily deal in books but also trade in ephemera, clothing, bats and caps. Added to this are the private deals, the ubiquitous charity auctions and finally the massive online trading conducted via eBay. As well, and new since 2008, is the rise of marketplaces and collector forums on social media, especially Facebook.

Individual athletes can liaise directly with collectors via their own social media platforms such as X (formerly Twitter) and Instagram: in total, the market is worth millions of dollars a year. The new market of limited edition or manufactured cricket memorabilia, which was once confined to collectables such as port[50] and the occasional artwork,[51] was a massive industry in Australia and to a lesser extent in Britain in the two decades up to the global financial crisis of late 2008. This segment has declined for varying factors: perceived poor value, oversupply, quality issues and possibly simply a lack of wall space on behalf of collectors.

For many collectors, cricket caps are an important and desirable artefact, the pinnacle of a collection, and for many Australians the cap represents the ultimate in memorabilia of any sport. The chance to own an item that can usually only be earned, while a paradox proves all too tempting for many collectors. Passionate collectors repeatedly say they would never put on a baggy green, that this would be almost sacrilegious. The cap owner in general values the notion of the exclusivity of the cap, and many understand they are custodians rather than owners of a relic that should be cared for and passed on.

Most collectors have a love of the game and knowledge of its history, ethos and traditions, and the majority are players, coaches and administrators whose collecting of memorabilia is an expression of their passion for the game. Collecting is rarely a pragmatic pursuit based on the possibility of financial gain.

There are three types of cricket collectors. First are those who played the game at the highest level and have an appreciation of its history and legacy. Initially their collections would have started with their own items then been augmented with swapped pieces. This continues to grow after retirement. The second collector is a non-player who likes to associate themselves with success and is a collector of limited-edition memorabilia. They (generally collectors are male) surround themselves with images of successful people and are well-educated high achievers. The third type of collector is a student of history who has an affection for the game and its traditions. Their interest in collecting is an intertwining of this fascination for sport and history. They are voracious readers and accumulators of facts and statistics.

Reflecting on the private interest in caps, public collections are becoming more diverse and are growing in number. Discussions with private and public collectors suggest that a cap is the ultimate representation of a player and his career. The challenge that the State Library of South Australia set itself in the late 1980s to find Don Bradman's cap is seen by some as the starting point of the cap's recent elevation. The library had an excellent collection of Bradman memorabilia, and following renovations had room to adorn the collection with a prized cap.

The best collection of baggy greens is held at the Melbourne Cricket Ground (MCG). The caps are part of the collection of the Melbourne Cricket Club (Melbourne CC), which has a separate museum, and the Australian Gallery of Sport and Olympic Museum (AGOSOM), which was opened in 1986. This building was demolished and the two collections came under the umbrella of the National Sports Museum (NSM), which was renamed the Australian Sports Museum (ASM) in 2019. In 2008 the Melbourne CC had 12 caps: Bill Woodfull 1928–29, Lindsay Hassett 1948, Clarrie Grimmett 1932–33, Keith Rigg 1936–37, Leo O'Brien 1936–37, Richie Benaud 1958–59, Neil Harvey 1961, Peter Burge 1964, Greg Chappell 1970s and Rod Marsh 1982–83.

It now has 26 caps, 24 in the Melbourne CC collection and an additional two as part of the AGOSOM collection. Some of the additions include Bert Ironmonger 1931, Len Darling 1936–37 and Ray Lindwall 1950–51. The museum acknowledges that its sole women's cap, worn by Betty Wilson 1947–48 and 1957–58, is an underrepresentation in the collection.

Adding relevance to the collections is the fact that the Australian Cricket Hall of Fame, whose inductees are announced each year at the Allan Border Medal function, is a Melbourne CC initiative. Many of the caps in the collection belonged to inductees of the hall of fame: some were donated and others bought. They range chronologically from 1928–29 to the recent commemoratives of 2000 and 2001. All caps are important to the different museums, and each has a different story to tell in context with that museum's charter. The Melbourne CC collection is based on the social history of sport.[52] The hall of fame obviously concentrates on the inductees and the NSM is dedicated to the display and interpretation of 20 sports, with emphasis on Olympic Games, Australian rules football and cricket.

The NSM opened at the MCG in March 2008 and contained a Baggy Green Room, which housed a majority of the cap collection. The NSM incorporates the Australian Cricket Hall of Fame, the Sport Australia Hall of Fame and the Olympic exhibition. The Melbourne CC oversees these various collections and their acquisitions policy is not based on emotion but relevance: such things as how the story of a particular cap relates to the ground, its members and or cricket in general. The overriding factors are the cap's provenance, its condition and relevance.[53]

The Bradman Museum at Bowral has a number of The Don's caps, significantly the 1936–37 Test cap Sir Donald gave to the museum, a South Australian Cricket Association cap from 1935 and a New South Wales cap that was purchased from the original recipient, who had been given the cap by Bradman in 1939.

The museum's former curator David Wells explained the collection: 'The Bradman Museum seeks out caps for inclusion in its collection as we regard them as the most potent symbol of cricket achievement, regardless of the standard. Obviously the baggy green, with its long tradition as the pinnacle of Australian cricket, is the most desirable of all, but we collect other caps as well, as they also inform our knowledge of the game.'

Wells also noted that the baggy style is particular to cricket and that caps are valued by the players over any other cricket equipment. He said that caps tell us first and foremost which club or team a player represented and at what level, while dated baggy greens tell us during what Test series they were used. The cut of the baggy green tells us that Australia developed the confidence after World War I to establish a design more suited to our climate and indicate a distancing from mother England.

The Bradman Museum has long displayed numerous caps as a part of its baggy green collection, many on loan. Those owned by the museum include Ashley Mallett's, one donated by manager Fred Bennett and two caps from female players Kit Raymond (2004) and Lindsay Reeler (1985). The most recent acquisition and one explored further in Chapter 13 is Shane Warne's bushfire auction cap.

The State Library of South Australia's Mortlock collection housed many items donated by Sir Donald Bradman; however, it did not have a cap. The quest for Bradman caps resulted in the library displaying over the years three of his baggy greens. Sir Donald gave his 1928 cap to his neighbours the Dunhams in the 1950s. The cap loaned to the library by son Peter Dunham went on display when the collection was reopened by John Bradman in November 2003. This cap famously came to market in 2020.

Collector John Kirkness with his Australian cricket helmet, as featured in The Sydney Morning Herald's Money supplement 'Collect' in 2006. (Fairfax)

Bradman gave his 1934 cap to Jack Bahan, a friend and golfing partner, in the 1930s. His grandson David Brown loaned the library the cap, which went on display in 1992. Kevin Truscott gave the library the 1948 cap Sir Donald had given to his father, Edgar Truscott. In his role as assistant manager at the London office of the Union Bank of Australia, Edgar helped Bradman with his banking during the 1948 tour. This cap was presented to the library at the SACA Test dinner in November 2004.[54]

Private collectors show similar discretion and passion. David Frith, a respected author and long-time collector, acquired his first baggy green in 1969: 'The first Australian Test cap I acquired was Ted McDonald's, and this was, I think, in 1969, in the north of England, in an antiques arcade. McDonald's 1921 cap, which is badly worn about the peak and has a few moth-holes, is [an] English "skull cap" design. It is also quite small, but I understand that this is the result of the passing of the years; shrinkage is unavoidable. It was made by Rowan Glasgow [author's note: the UK manufacture explains the English shape]. Grimmett's 1924–25 is faded but otherwise in good condition. It is slightly baggy in design. I bought the first three and was given the last two: McDonald, Clarrie Grimmett [1924–25], Gil Langley [1953], Jeff Thomson [1977] and Allan Border [1989].'[55]

Why did David collect baggy greens? 'They are particularly significant items in my large collection of memorabilia,' he said. Given that his collection comprised thousands of pieces, this is a significant statement about the cap's status.

Frith noted changes in attitudes towards collecting baggy greens since 1969: 'They simply weren't to be found in those days, except in the rare instance when one might have been presented to a museum. There were no cricket auctions until the late 1970s. Gradually, former cricketers have overcome reluctance to part with the caps: they fetch big money, and some have several of them so why not? Of all a Test cricketer's attire, surely the cap is the most significant, treasured above all other items of clothing?'

In 2023 David started the process of selling his mammoth collection, including the baggy greens: some of which returned to Australian collectors.

Sydney collector John Kirkness, who was featured in *The Sydney Morning Herald*'s Money supplement,[56] said: 'When a kid dreams of playing for his country he dreams of a baggy green, not a floppy hat or Test shirts adorned with logo, initials and Test number.'

More caps from the Jason Brooks collection. (Image Michael Fahey)

Kirkness believes the refusal by Cricket Australia to sell replicas is important. 'Cricket is unique in Australia and you cannot buy a replica cap, as you can with jerseys for other national teams such as the Kangaroos, Wallabies and Socceroos. A BG is desirable, irrespective of who played in it. Certainly a cap is more valuable depending on the player but there is definite kudos with a cap before you add the player's additional charisma. I did like it when the series was listed on the cap; in that way you could directly relate the events of a series with a player – there was a historical link.'

With dates no longer printed on caps, Kirkness would like to see the player number on the cap as is done with England caps and the Australian One Day International caps. He still owns the one baggy green cap and several Australian helmets, though he recently added one of the miniature presentation boxed baggy greens to his collection. He also collects New South Wales caps, as they too have rarely changed. (Apparently there have been only two badges worn on New South Wales caps since the middle part of the 19th century.) This, Kirkness says, adds to the New South Wales cap's significance and desirability: 'All the other states have changed their caps and emblem; some many times over.'

Brisbane collector Harry Wszola, who in 2007 had a full-sized cap and one of the miniature presentation caps, has added two more to the collection since. He believes that the heritage of Australian sport should be preserved through collecting. As well as cricket, he acquires collectables from many sports. His motivation is to ensure that his children and their descendants appreciate the sportsmen of the past, understanding the sacrifices many made to reach the top.

Wszola shelved his sporting career for academic studies and relates to the struggle of those who excelled in the amateur era and received little monetary compensation – if any – for their endeavours. He doesn't consider the monetary value of the caps, as he doesn't buy them for resale. The same rule will apply for his descendants when it is their turn to be the custodians of the caps.

Like death and taxes, one sure thing is that every collector is merely a custodian of these wonderful artefacts. Every person's life changes and evolves and their collecting can wax, wane and sometimes pause. Almost inevitably the collecting will cease for the family unless the antecedent's passion is passed on like a baton to the next generation. More often, though, given that passions are highly personal, is that the bug doesn't run in the family and some form of dispersal is required.

While some collections cease, others commence. One such newcomer is Jason Brooks, a friend of Stephen Waugh. In 2021, 32 Australian caps were assembled for an exhibition at Sydney's Hyatt Regency Hotel to accompany Steve Waugh's Spirit of Cricket photographs and book. While some notable caps were from the Sydney Cricket Ground, including one of Bradman's along with Steve Waugh's own cap, more than 20 were from Jason's impressive collection. These included seven Australian captains

Part of the amazing collection of caps in the office of Craig Hawkins. (Image courtesy of Craig Hawkins)

and several hall of fame members. Jason doesn't call himself a collector, preferring to be known as a 'custodian'. He said: 'I am like any kid of my era: everyone wanted to play Test cricket for Australia. I always wanted to have a baggy green and play for Australia. There is only one reason I didn't: I just wasn't good enough.'

Asked to pick the most important cap, he nominated Richie Benaud's: 'A great Australian captain, which he probably doesn't get the kudos for . . . For his commentating, he's a household name. To own a cap of someone who was in everyone's living room every night.'

Another major collector to emerge since 2007 is Craig Hawkins, whose stockpile totals well over 700: this is believed to be a world record. There are 24 baggy greens in his collection. 'Why? I guess partly because I can. The game has given me so much, and the collection is a small way of honouring the players and the experiences that went before me. Each cap has a story . . . from the interesting, to the historic, to the obscure . . . Discovering what happened behind the cap is often as interesting as the details of the people, and the matches the caps were worn in.

Collector Neil Mumford and friends enjoying his substantial baggy green collection. (Image courtesy of Neil Mumford)

'Without realising, I seem to have a disproportionate number of wicket-keepers in my collection, which leans towards my own days behind the stumps many years ago. I'm not sure I have a favourite, but the Ben Barnett 1938 Ashes cap is special, as it was the last tour before the war and Barnett only played four Test matches in all on that tour. I have a number of Barry Jarman caps, plus his miniature, and I have Len Maddocks' baggy green and his wicket-keeping gloves, which make a nice set.

'I have three baggy greens from the Invincibles, Ron Hamence [1948], Sam Loxton [1949–50] and Neil Harvey [1954–55]. Then there are caps from players who are quite rightfully considered "legends": Alan Davidson [1957–58], Doug Walters [1967–68], Rod Marsh and Allan Border. And I also have a Greg Matthews cap [that] is special because I played New South Wales Combined High Schools with Greg in 1977. Each cap is special, however, because they all represent so much.'

The most conscientious of collectors, Hawkins has set in place arrangements for the collection to be looked after by business successors and family. 'It is like the game itself: the collection will grow and evolve over time, and I trust the cricketing gods to make sure it is well looked after. There is way too much history involved.'

The final recent baggy gatherer provides a neat closing of the circle. Neil Mumford, also a collector of all cricket memorabilia, has amassed 14 Australian caps from 1921 to 1993. He advised that the initial 2008 release of this book piqued his interest in caps and led to him starting a collection.

His favourites are Ted a'Beckett's 1928 and 1930 caps. This is an interesting choice given Neil's collection includes those worn by many of the game's legends. Ted a' Beckett played just four Test matches but was the unsung partner and witness to two monumental accomplishments. When Don Bradman scored his maiden Test match 100 at the MCG in 1928 Ted was at the non-striker's end. Likewise, when Bradman scored his 334 in 1930 Ted was once again at the other end.

MF

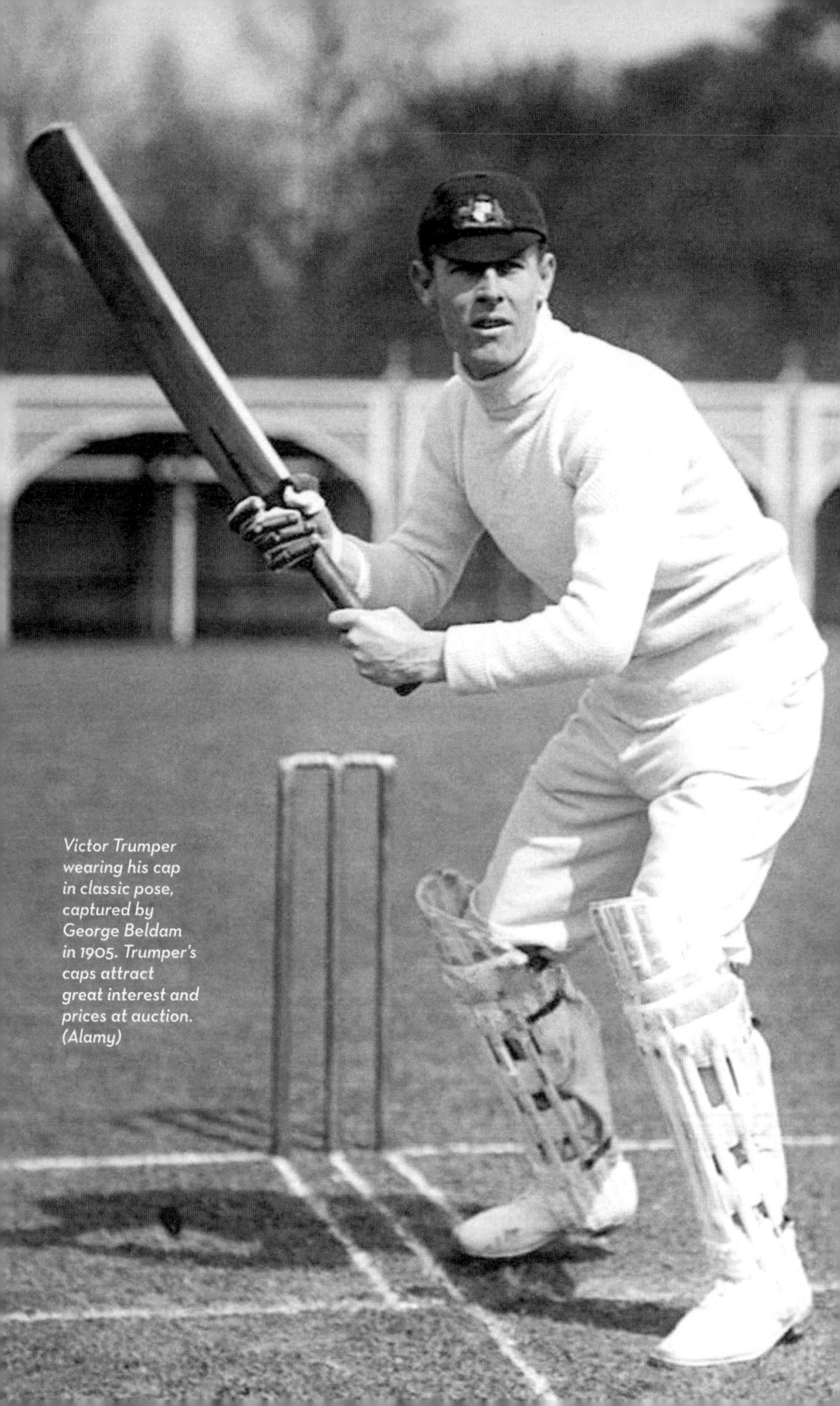

Victor Trumper wearing his cap in classic pose, captured by George Beldam in 1905. Trumper's caps attract great interest and prices at auction. (Alamy)

CHAPTER 5

Values

The idea of a baggy green having monetary value is a recent phenomenon. Before the first sports auction held by Phillips in London in 1978 caps were generally not bought and sold but swapped or given away, perhaps reappearing in flea markets or antique stores. Caps had great value to players because they had to earn them with good performances, but they had no monetary value as no market existed for sports memorabilia. The rise of sports auctions, websites and electronic auctions meant that a market for caps has substantially grown.

Over the 16 years to 2008 there were 185 offerings of baggy greens for sale. There is now reliable data for 139 sales, while the rest were passed in or sold privately after the auction. This information comes mainly from the major auction houses and sports specialists, and with some sales figures from retailers and charity events.

The total value of those 139 sales is $2,275,477 (all financial figures are in Australian dollars unless otherwise specified, and figures vary slightly from the 2008 edition due to subsequently discovered sales data). After excluding one cap sold at a testimonial and donated back, the average of these sales is $16,162 a cap. The five Bradman caps, which averaged almost $160,000 a sale, have attracted much higher prices than other

The extraordinary Craig Hawkins collection of Australian caps, including multiple baggy greens. (Image courtesy of Craig Hawkins)

caps so they are excluded from this calculation. Bradman caps aside, baggy greens have sold for an average price of $9,909.

As of November 2023 there had been 313 sales since the first recorded pair of caps sold in 1988. The latest 174 sales from 2008 to 2023 reached a total value of $3,101,713, with an average of $17,825. Removing the eight outlier sales in that period results in 166 sales for a total of $1,803,500, with an average of $10,864. The year 2008 was the peak of the surge that started in 1999, with the global financial crisis (GFC) of late 2008 seeing values fall then tumble in the following six years. From 2016 the market rose, and 2023 was a highpoint for the number of caps sold and amounts achieved.

A better measure or current value is the four years from 2020 to 2023: 34 caps were sold, with an average of $14,426.

Leski Auctions' December 2008 auction featured Bradman's 1948 cap. (Image courtesy of Michael Fahey)

In the 2008 edition the major dealers in baggy greens were listed; in this edition the dealers and their sales numbers have been updated. The new figures show that, like collectors, auction houses also come and go. Leski Auctions in Melbourne had offered 48 caps, then this rose to 103 by 2023. They also traded as Mossgreen from 2014 to 2017 and sold another 12 in that period. Christie's Australia sold 28 caps but no longer offer sports auctions, Ludgrove's sold 20 caps and are also no longer trading, while Knight's Sporting Auctions in Britain had sold 46 caps by 2023. Others in Australia are Lawsons with six sales, Sports Memorabilia Australia/Legends Genuine Memorabilia with 33, Icons of Sports with two and Framous and Bonhams & Goodman with three. Newcomers Abacus Auctions have sold 12, Sportsonline six and Leonard Joel two. In Britain, Graham Budd Auctions have sold six caps, Mullock Madeley Auctions six, Bonham & Brook/Bonham three and T. Vennett-Smith Auctions three.

Most of these sales were conducted at public auctions. The cap of a 'modestly performed' Test player generally retails for between $5,000 and $9,000, while the cap of a high-profile player can command $15,000 to $25,000. What have been some of the highlights over the years? In ascending order, the record prices achieved have been as listed chronologically on page 81.

SALE YEAR	PLAYER AND SERIES YEAR/S
1988	Grimmett, 1932–33
1995	Bradman, 1946–47 (first cap from that series)
1997	Walters, 1974
1997	Trumper, 1899
1998	Grimmett, 1930
1999	Woodfull, 1932–33
2000	Oldfield, 1932–33
2002	Miller, 1953
2003	Bradman, 1947–48
2003	Bradman, 1946–47 (second cap from that series)
2003	Bradman, 1948
2004	Trumper, 1907
2004	Bradman, 1930
2005	Morris, 1948
2005	Bradman, 1946–47 (first cap from that series again)
2006	Miller, 1954–55
2008	Bradman, 1948
2016	Richardson, 1932–33
2017	Bradman, 1934
2018	Oldfield, 1932–33
2020	Bradman, 1928–29

OTHER	TRUMPER	BRADMAN
$1,200		
		$7,500
$4,232		
	$28,750	
$7,475		
$23,000		
$28,000		
$35,250		
		$180,000
		$88,835
		$425,000
	$94,000	
		$95,385
$40,000		
		$95,400
$40,775		
		$468,913
$53,725		
		$148,800
$67,100		
		$474,750

The big names of Bradman, Trumper and Miller and the big series of 1932–33 and 1948 still command the highest prices.

Another way to gauge price increases over time is to compare the amount realised when the same cap has appeared a number of times. For example, Colin McDonald's 1956 cap sold at Leski Auctions in 1999 for $2,990 then at Knight's in 2002 for $6,571 and again at Knight's in 2005 for $7,896, which represents a 264 per cent increase in six years. In 2010 the impact of the GFC was evident when the cap sold again: this time for $4,923. Wally Grout's 1962–63 cap sold at Phillips in 2000 for $7,200 and at Leski four years later for $31,455: a 436 per cent increase. Don Tallon's 1950–51 cap sold at Ludgrove's in 2003 for $7,000 then two years later at Leski for $12,815: a 183 per cent increase.

How do baggy green prices compare with similar items such as helmets and One Day International (ODI) caps? In the eight years up to 2007 only 11 ODI caps were sold, for an average price of $1,850. The World Series Cricket (WSC) caps worn in super Tests and one-day matches have fared a little better, averaging $2,750 for the four sold. By 2023 a total of 39 yellow baggy/ODI caps had sold, at an average of $1,426. The explosion of ODI games and the easy availability of these caps – as opposed to Test caps – has seen the prices for more recent ODI caps fall.

Leski's September 2008 auction featured five baggy greens. (Image courtesy of Michael Fahey)

Since 2007 WSC had been seen in a more favourable light. In 2014 Cricket Australia announced that statistics from these super Tests would be recognised in a separate category, essentially a first class classification. With some agitation they may be upgraded again to Test status. As of early 2024, nine WSC yellow caps had sold at an average of $3,296.

As of 2007 there had been 14 Australian blazers sold at an average price of $2,990. The best price achieved was $8,225, for Keith Miller's 1953 tour blazer. By 2023 this number had risen to 34, with the highest amount being $122,000 for Bradman's blazer from 1936–37.

The 1899 Trumper cap was the first to attract a significant price at auction. It is one of the few pre-1920s caps to ever come to market. (Image courtesy of Legends Genuine Memorabilia)

Excluding this sale, the longer-term average is a comparable $2,900. The highest non-Bradman item was Alan Kippax's 1932–33 blazer, which fetched $11,500.

As of 2007 Test sweaters averaged $745 from nine sales, and Test shirts averaged $1,500 from four sales. By 2023, 21 sweaters had sold for an average of $1,163. This figure was bolstered by the sale of Warren Bardsley's 1921 sweater in 2018 for $6,801.

In 2007 green and yellow helmets attracted less interest. Twelve had been offered for sale, with estimates ranging from $600 for Ray Bright's to $5,000 for Mark Waugh's. There have been no sales apart from the auction of a significant helmet worn by Steve Waugh when he made 200 in the West Indies in 1995. The helmet was signed by the squad and offered with signed batting gloves used in the innings, and it sold for $11,500.

As predicted the demand for helmets has grown, given the paucity of baggy green caps. Sixteen green helmets have now sold at an average of $3,376, with $4,484 paid for Steve Waugh's 1995 Ashes helmet. Shane Warne's 1993 Ashes helmet auctioned at Leski in August 2022 five months after his death and achieved $10,157. Clearly, the baggy green has commanded a significant premium over other items of cricket apparel.

The prices for variations of the baggy green design are interesting. Three baggy whites from the 1988 Bicentennial Test had sold up to 2008 for an average of $4,075, and a further cap sold in 2010 for $5,690. (It should be noted that both the Australian and England teams received caps and they were not match worn.) A player's 2000 millennium cap sold in 2004 for $15,000, and it remains the only one to come to market. Five of the 2003 presentation miniature caps have sold, with an average of $2,475.

Don Bradman (left) and Bill Ponsford (right) in 1934 upon setting a record 451 batting partnership.

What are the trends and implications for the market in the future? From 2004 to 2009 the average price per cap based on 50 sales was $13,517; from 1997 to 2003 it was $7,930 based on 78 sales. Therefore, caps almost doubled in value in 10 years. In 2008 the market peaked, then went into free fall in 2010 for four years. The average for the 13 years from 2010 to 2022 saw 105 caps sell at an average of $8,784, almost back to the value as the year 2000.

Significantly, in 2023 16 caps were sold for a record $16,129 apiece. What does this tell us? In basic terms, the values are increasing, and they depend on the player whose cap is being sold, the year and series and the condition of the cap. However, the market as a whole is affected by macro-economic factors such as the GFC. The passing of time also plays a role. Trumper's first cap, from the important 1899 series, sold for $28,750 in 1997. The next, from 1907, went for a hammer price of $83,000 in 2004 or close to $94,000 with buyer's premium added. Speculation suggested the 1899 cap might achieve $100,000 in the current market.

Christie's South Kensington auction in June 2004 featured Bradman's cap. (Image courtesy of Michael Fahey)

Keith Miller's caps have also grown in value. In 1999 his 1952–53 cap sold for $8,700. In 2002 his 1953 cap brought $35,200; in 2006 his 1954–55 baggy went for $40,775; and his 1956 cap for $29,125. The last cap had minor wear holes in the brim. No Miller cap has come to market since or been sold since 2006. Miller had a great series against the West Indies in 1954–55, with 20 wickets and 439 runs, and this was reflected in the price achieved for that cap.

Many people lament the sale of caps, believing that an item earned or given as a gift should not be sold. These are reasonable reservations, but a market cannot be prohibited and some ethics can coexist with the sale of caps. Some recipients or their children have returned caps to the cricketer or his descendants. In one case a player had given his cap away years before and then a descendant of the original beneficiary wished to sell it. The dealer, feeling uneasy that a gift was being profited from, ensured that the player received a cut from his commission of the sale.

What motivates a person to buy a certain cap? A collector may wish to have one from a certain series or it may have belonged to a favourite player. The motivation is different for each so predicting the result of individual sales is difficult: it depends on who is looking to buy at the time.

Some caps were not included in this analysis. The Bradman caps, which are dealt with later, were excluded because of the huge prices they have attracted. Another excluded was the cap belonging to Greg Matthews, which was auctioned at a testimonial organised by his manager Max Markson in December 1998. The cap was sold for $45,000 and was returned to Matthews by the bidder, Carl Howell, the head of Advanced Hair Studios, for whom Matthews was an advertising star.[57] The price was vastly more than expected, which can't be fully explained by the charity element of the auction. Research revealed that from sale proceeds of more than $200,000 at the function, a modest $10,000 was donated to charity.

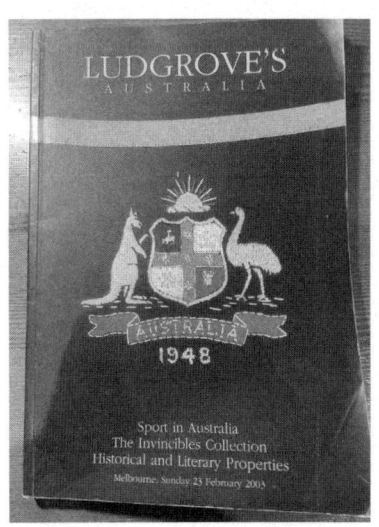

Ludgrove's Australia's February 2003 auction was a bonanza, with Arthur Morris's 1948 cap, Loxton and Bradman's 1947-48 caps and five of Ashley Mallet's caps all featuring. (Image courtesy of Michael Fahey)

Of more interest than the tax-free payment Matthews received from the auction was the question posed by Phillip Koch, a journalist from *The Sunday Telegraph*. He suggested that the sale by Matthews had caused consternation but acknowledged that the recent sales of Olympic and Commonwealth Games medals of Betty Cuthbert, Raelene Boyle and Dawn Fraser, while unusual for sport, were just catching up with the long-established trade in bravery medals, including Victoria Crosses. The sale of the Mike Whitney cap in 1993 was cited as the only other recent sale of a baggy green.

Reacting to the Matthews sale, Steve Waugh said: 'I don't consider my cap to be memorabilia. It's something to treasure. It will be passed on to my family.'[58]

Matthews expected criticism for selling his cap. 'If there's "x" amount of people out there having difficulty comprehending where I'm coming from, I apologise for that,' he said, 'but Greg Matthews is 100 per cent happy within himself.'[59]

Where do prices go from here? Research and experience confirm that most collectors are cricket lovers, that large, speculative investment has not arrived, although there is potential for this to develop and especially with an item as prestigious as the baggy green. Some reasons for this potential include an increase in the knowledge of how many caps are in circulation and who has them, increased availability of funds from superannuation, the interest shown by five major collecting institutions in Australia and reduced supply, given that since the mid-1990s players have been limited to one cap.

The examples of world soccer and US baseball memorabilia might seem stratospheric, but what is to stop speculative investors becoming interested in cricket memorabilia?

This quote comes from the 2008 edition of this book and is reprinted to show what changes occurred from 2007 to 2023 in overseas markets, and how the newer values compare with those we thought were high in 2007.

> *In 2002 Pele's 1970 Brazilian World Cup shirt sold for £157,750 and Sir Geoff Hurst's 1966 England World Cup-winning shirt reached $263,120. The bat Sir Garfield Sobers used to hit the record six sixes in an over at Cardiff in 1968 sold at Christies for $146,875, and Shane Gould's 1972 Munich Olympics diary was bought for $41,125 by the NSW State Library.*
>
> *In the US, baseball dominates the sports auction rooms. The Holy Grail of card collecting is the Honus Wagner 1910 trade card. The Pittsburgh Pirates shortstop had the card pulled from distribution as a cigarette card as he opposed smoking. This extremely rare card has sold for as much as $US1.265 million. Recent legal cases over baseballs hit for home run records have highlighted the extremes people will go to because of the money involved. Mark McGwire's 1998 70th home run ball sold for $US3.2 million while in 2003 the 73rd home run ball of Barry Bonds sold for $US450,000.*

Vic Richardson at Lord's in 1930. (Alamy)

A Honus Wagner card sold in August 2022 for US$7.25 million, although this is not the highest amount for a trading card. In August 2022 a 1952 Topps mint condition Mickey Mantle card was sold by Heritage Auctions for US$12.6 million.

Shirt and jersey values overseas have also exploded. Michael Jordan's 1998 NBA Finals Game 1 Chicago Bulls jersey sold for US$10.91 million in September 2022, and Maradona's Hand of God Argentina shirt from the 1986 World Cup quarter final achieved US$9.28 million in May 2022.

In 2008 we stated that given the increased prices achieved recently and the increasing age of many caps prices for baggy greens should rise, especially for caps from great players or from famous series such as 1920–21, the Bodyline series 1932–33, the Invincibles in 1948 and the team's run of 16 consecutive Test wins to March 2001 and a further 16 successive victories to January 2008. At 2008 the sales of 1932–33 Bodyline caps was around $20,000. Recent sales to that date had been Bert Oldfield's cap in 2000 for $28,200, Bill Woodfull's cap in 2003 for $23,000 and Vic Richardson's for $20,125.

Subsequent sales saw a dramatic uplift. The Richardson cap came to market again in 2016, with estimates of £12,000 to £18,000. It sold for a hammer amount of £21,000 or the equivalent of AU$53,725, including buyer's premium. Likewise, Oldfield's cap re-entered the market in 2018 with estimates of $40,000 to $60,000 and achieved AU$67,100.

Only 18 caps dating from before 1940 were sold publicly in the 20 years from 1988 to 2008, but others may have been held in private collections and sold privately. Significantly, 15 of these were sold before 2003. Prices have doubled since: at 2008 the average for caps from the pre-1940 era was $15,335, but many of these sold way back in the 1990s. As of early 2024

Famous baggy greens worn by Australian cricket captains (left to right) Victor Trumper, Don Bradman and Steve Waugh on display at the SCG in Sydney in 2011. (Newspix)

Steve Waugh's 1995 West Indies Tour helmet. (JPG)

there have been 38 sales for pre-1940 caps, and since 2007 these sales – excluding Trumper and Bradman caps – have averaged $25,479.

In 2008 only five caps from before 1930 had been sold, then as of early 2024 there had been an additional five sales for a total of just 10. They are rare indeed.

MF

Schoolteacher Cam Tinley with his Don Bradman 1946–47 baggy green cricket cap he bought at auction in 1995. (Newspix)

CHAPTER 6

The Taj Mahal of baggy greens

Don Bradman bestrode the game like a colossus. He set numerous records, affected the game's laws and history and has even affected the way memorabilia is collected.

An examination of Bradman's Test caps – what he did with them, where they ended up, how they have been marketed and the prices they attract at auction – provides a wonderful kaleidoscope of the baggy green market. This saga includes auctioneers, media corporations, a prime minister and his Goods and Services Tax (GST),[60] museums, valuers, wealthy buyers, lucky sellers, perceptive investors and generous individuals.

When discussion turns to memorabilia, especially baggy green caps, the main question is: 'What is it worth?' The mainstream press has a fascination with the dollar value of caps and the increase in their prices over the years. This is understandable as it is an easy way to measure interest; however, price is not always an indication of an item's value or desirability. Many artefacts from cricket's so-called golden age, from the 1890s to 1915, appeal to only a small selection of enthusiasts. The general public has fleeting knowledge of the players from this period, and apart from the giants of that era W.G. Grace and Victor Trumper there is not a great deal of public interest in its history and memorabilia.

Sir Donald Bradman's legacy transcends his unsurpassed record as a player, administrator and selector and his fame has fired the public's interest in the cricket and cricketers from the 1920s. His eminence and longevity have ensured that many tens of thousands of cricket fans have read and continue to read about his life and the cricketers intertwined in it. In doing so, the general public is familiar with cricket events from almost 100 years ago. In Australia this depth of knowledge does not occur in other sports, probably not even in politics or general history. Unwitting participants in Bradman's career are known half a world and half a century away: English cricketer Eric Hollies, with a modest Test career, is almost as well known in Australia as Test hero Harold Larwood and his Bodyline captain Douglas Jardine. Conversely, very few Australians could name the national rugby union or rugby league captains from the 1930s, let alone those from Britain.

Even Bradman's recollections of cricket in his youth are a powerful statement on the game. His praise of Charlie Macartney's innings of 170 at the SCG in 1921, the first Test the-then 12-year-old Bradman had

The Australian cricket team hold a minute's silence with baggy greens over their hearts to show respect for the legendary Keith Miller, who died on 11 October 2004. The team playing in Chennai wore black armbands for the first day of the match in tribute. (Newspix)

attended, was influential in the successful campaign to have Macartney inducted into the Australian Cricket Hall of Fame in 2007. The growth of the memorabilia industry, the continued interest – or obsession, some would argue – with Sir Donald Bradman and the re-evaluation of the baggy green's legacy were reflected in the 2003 marketing, auction and sale of Bradman's 1946–47 and 1948 baggy greens.

The near deification of Bradman has been espoused by ex–prime minister John Howard: 'So he was more than just a great cricketer and great sportsman; he was a dominant Australian personality in a way [that] I don't think any other person has been in the last 100 years. Sir Donald Bradman's contribution was more than to the game of cricket. It was his role in the history and development of Australia that will also be remembered. No individual has so inspired successive generations of Australians across such a breadth of age, geography and circumstances as Sir Donald.'[61]

The outpouring of public grief at Bradman's passing in 2001 enabled a remarkable marketing campaign to be orchestrated, all centred on a Bradman cap. With the baggy green now so high in the public's esteem, several caps were marketed by former Christie's Australia auctioneer Michael Ludgrove and former Australian Cricket Board CEO Graham Halbish, who formed the short-lived but headline-grabbing auction house Ludgrove's. Two Bradman caps smashed records, caused a certain amount of intrigue and gained international attention, yet both never went under the hammer.

In 2003 News Limited (now News Corp), in conjunction with Ludgrove's, launched a public appeal in its nationwide stable of newspapers. As proclaimed on the front pages, the aim was to 'Bring the 1948 baggy green home'. With an obvious nationalist pitch, an appeal for $500,000 was launched – the price then of a substantial family home – just for a cricket cap. This appeal attracted financial support for Cricket Australia[62] and generated huge publicity for the proposed auction, which was to be held by Ludgrove's in London in June. Was $500,000 unreasonable? The only way to answer that is to examine other Bradman caps in museums and their history at auction.

From 1995 to 2003 collectors witnessed an increase in the reported sale price of a Bradman cap. According to *The Wisden Book of Cricket Memorabilia* (Lennard Publishing, 1990), the big auction houses began to specialise in cricket memorabilia in 1978, then came Marylebone Cricket

Club's 1987 bicentennial auction, a blockbuster that set numerous records. Not long after the birth of large auctioning of cricket memorabilia, the first Bradman cap was put up for sale.

On 22 September 1995 Christie's at South Kensington, London offered his 1946–47 cap. It was listed simply as: 'BRADMAN, Sir Donald George – An Australian cap in green embroidered with the Australian crest and legends "Australia. 1946–47", with a card stapled to the brim inscribed in Bradman's hand: "To Tim Biles. From Don Bradman" (torn and creased) PROVENANCE: The Revd. Cannon Timothy Biles – see footnote to lot 87.' The estimate was £300 to £500, and this was well and truly shattered with a final bid of £3,375 (AU$7,800 at the time). This cap, the 'Biles' 1946–47 cap, (the need for a distinction over and above the year will be explained later) was bought by Western Australian school teacher Cameron Tingley.

Only two other Bradman caps were in the public domain at the time, and both had been given away by Sir Donald. He had given his 1934 cap to Jack Bahen, a friend and golfing partner, in the late 1930s. Bahen's grandson David Brown gave the cap to the State Library of South Australia for a long-term loan, and it had been displayed briefly in 1992. The other cap was Sir Donald's 1936–37 baggy green, which he had donated to the Bradman Museum in 1993. No other Bradman caps emerged for another eight years, then in a 21-month period to November 2004 another six caps were offered at Christie's and Ludgrove's or loaned to the State Library of South Australia.

To date, there are nine Bradman caps in the public domain and each one's journey from Sir Donald to the current owner provides an interesting story. There may be others that have been in private hands and only a select few know of their existence. How many are there? This is a difficult question, given that players were often issued with two caps per tour. The existence of two caps per player for the home series in 1946–47 and the possibility that this happened in other home series means there might be more Bradman baggy greens than historians and experts have estimated. The swapping of caps among teammates has clouded the quest to locate every Bradman baggy. Time may reveal the correct number as more caps are unearthed and original contracts tell us how many caps each player received.

The first of the six new Bradman baggies to surface was from the 1947–48 series against India in Australia; it was offered by Ludgrove's at

Bradman in cap utilising his famous drive. (Newspix)

an auction in Melbourne in February 2003. In stark contrast to the paucity of description for the first cap auctioned, the 1946–47 cap at Christie's in 1995, this auction's catalogue information ran to three pages with four photographs, yet little information about the provenance of the cap was published, although the catalogue said that 'detailed letter of provenance signed by the vendor is available'. Estimates of between $100,000 and

$200,000 were a huge increase over the previous public auction amount of $7,800 that had been achieved eight years earlier.

Ludgrove's' publicity saw pre-auction reports in News Limited's *The Sunday Telegraph* and *The Australian*. These papers announced expectations of $500,000 and between $200,000 and $250,000 respectively. However, the cap did not reach auction but, according to Ludgrove's, was sold by private treaty before the auction. Although the amount was not disclosed because of a confidentiality clause the auction house did suggest it had been more than $180,000, the previous record for a Bradman item: a life-sized Bradman statue.

With such an increase surely this record would stand for years, but that was not to be. Ludgrove's began a campaign to sell the Holy Grail of caps: Bradman's 1948 Invincibles cap. Here was the last Test cap worn by the game's greatest player on the only undefeated Ashes tour by an Australian team. On 21 May 2003 all major News Limited papers began a front-page quest to reclaim an Australian treasure that was to be auctioned by Ludgrove's in Britain in July. One paper declared: '*The Daily Telegraph* is determined that cricket's most famous cap should be returned to Australia and displayed for posterity.'

The first Bradman cap to come to market was given to Tim Biles. He's shown with Bradman's cap, blazer and bat. (Image courtesy of Michael Fahey)

The number of a bank account was listed and the public were invited to donate to the appeal to buy the cap. The vendor, Richard Robins, Sir Donald's godson, then offered the newspaper's Australian appeal an exclusive option to buy before auction; expectations were for a price of more than $500,000.

The Australian Cricket Board donated $10,000 to the fund and many great names endorsed the appeal. As reported on the ABC television program *Media Watch*, Ricky Ponting, Keith Stackpole, Allan Border, Sir Donald's son John Bradman, Merv Hughes and even Bali bomb victim and AFL player Jason McCartney supported the appeal. McCartney was quoted in *The Mercury* as saying: 'The cap definitely should come back home. It is a unique piece of Australian history.'

A lone dissenting voice was the Australian Test captain Steve Waugh: 'To me, there are more important causes to raise money for,' he said, after discussing with *The Sydney Morning Herald* his involvement in charity work in India. Three weeks of choreographed appeals met with limited success, and on 11 June 2003 the *Herald Sun*, *The Mercury*, *The Advertiser* and *The Daily Telegraph* appealed for more donations, saying that 'the quest to raise $500,000 has not met with the spontaneous response expected'.

A month before the Ludgrove's auction another Bradman cap, surprisingly a second 1946–47 cap marked 'D.G. Bradman', was auctioned by Christie's in Britain. As the Tim Biles 1946–47 cap had been sold in 1995, also by Christie's, how was there another cap? *The Age*[63] interviewed Christie's marketing consultant Rick Pike, who was 'quite satisfied' the cap was the one originally presented to Bradman and worn by him for most of the series. It was a small cap that matched Bradman's size. Pike said the Tim Biles cap was a second or a replacement. 'Somewhere along the line, Bradman has used a spare. There were many documented cases of Australian international players using spare caps during series in the 40's,' he said.

Further clouding the issue were reports in *The Sydney Morning Herald* that Keith Miller and Bradman swapped caps before the first Test of 1946–47 and kept them all summer. Quoting Miller from Britain's *Daily Mail*: 'You know how fastidious the Don was. That morning in Brisbane he fiddled around with the cap that he'd been given and complained it didn't fit, so I tossed him mine and said, "Try that." It fitted perfectly. He wore it throughout the series.' Miller believed that the two caps had the initials DGB and KRM written inside them and had no idea where his cap, with DGB, went.

Christie's were adamant that the cap was Bradman's[64] and said it had been handed to Ron Saggers, the Australian wicket-keeper, and then passed on to the present vendor. The controversy seems not to have deterred the eventual owner, an Australian living in London, who paid £35,250 (AU$88,835) for it. Given that amount, the expectations during Ludgrove's' 1948 cap campaign that it would sell for about $500,000 seemed ludicrously extravagant, even allowing for a premium for the association with the famous 1948 Invincibles tour.

On 7 July 2003 the ABC's *Media Watch* reported that one of its representatives had asked the National Australia Bank about the campaign account balance,[65] which was reported to be between $8,000 and $9,000. Obviously the appeal would not be buying the cap, so another buyer was required.

Unexpectedly, on 30 June 2003, just days after the 1946–47 Bradman cap achieved a public auction record of $88,000 in Britain, Ludgrove's announced that an unnamed New South Wales collector had paid $425,000 for the Invincibles cap. In the *Herald Sun* that day Halbish, the chairman of Ludgrove's, said: 'It is higher than the world record price of Sir Donald's 1947–48 Indian series baggy green that Ludgrove's sold before auction in February for an undisclosed sum. At that time, a Bradman sculpture sold for $180,000 was the yardstick.' Halbish added: 'News Limited's campaign showed that the people of Australia wanted the cap. They responded with spirit, but the private offer was too significant for the owner to refuse an immediate sale.'

In the reports carried by the *Herald Sun*, ABC Online and *The Sydney Morning Herald* of 30 June, the buyer was unnamed but identified as a former winner of *Who Wants to be a Millionaire*. 'The new owner is planning to put the cap on public display,' Halbish said.[66]

Given his exploits on national TV, the buyer was identified as Tim Serisier,[67] who had just won $250,000 on the popular quiz show. 'The Invincible cap belongs on public display and not in a bank vault,' he was quoted as saying. The cap did go on display, initially at some regional shopping centres,[68] and then becoming part of a road show presented by Cricket Australia and Travelex (a Cricket Australia sponsor) that visited capital cities and regional centres in early 2004.[69] A photograph of the cap sitting in a perspex box was featured in Cricket Australia's Insight newsletter.[70]

Surprisingly, News Limited offered refunds on any donations yet they claimed the campaign had been a success, because Serisier had learned about the cap through the newspapers' appeal.

In another interesting twist, Australia's most public cricket tragic John Howard and his new goods and services tax (GST) came into play. According to a report on dawn.com on 10 September 2003, before leaving to collect the cap in Britain Serisier asked the Australian Taxation Office and Australian customs if the cap would attract the 10 per cent GST.

The tax office responded that it probably would but then customs told him that a cap is a cap, which he took to mean the baggy green would be regarded as a piece of clothing and be exempt from the tax. Upon his return he was advised that he was liable for GST, so he paid it the day after his return. 'It's disappointing, because it will discourage Australian investors from bringing heritage items into this country,' Serisier said.

Based on the reported price of $425,000, the tax added $42,500. Thus the cap had cost almost the half a million dollars predicted.[71] According to *The Sydney Morning Herald*[72] the GST liability was due to the cap being a collectable item, which customs had advised. This was 'a view backed up by the Prime Minister John Howard, an avid cricket fan'.

Bradman's baggy green cap from 1948 went up for auction in Melbourne in 2008. (Newspix)

THE TAJ MAHAL OF BAGGY GREENS • 101

Rumour dogged Ludgrove's, especially when stories of auction irregularities relating to a bat signed by Grace and Bradman aired on the Nine network's *A Current Affair*. The former federal minister John Brown had consigned the bat to Ludgrove's with the aim of raising money for charity. The bat was knocked down at auction way below the reserve, and neither the new owner nor Ludgrove's were prepared to recompense Brown or the charity for the amount he believed it was worth. It was revealed that Michael Ludgrove had resigned as a director of the business, and in 2004 an administrator was appointed. Creditors subsequently accepted 30 cents in the dollar.

Six months after the auction the *Herald Sun*'s Spy reported that a London source close to the British vendor said the sale figure for the 1948 cap may have been $360,000. Subsequent investigation has led me to believe that an intermediary bought the cap from Ludgrove's for the lower figure, which was the amount used to pay out the vendor, then the cap was sold for the $425,000 pre-auction. Whatever the case, speculation was rife. Was the cap worth $425,000 (plus GST)? Would it have achieved a similar price in a public auction? Would subsequent pieces emulate this record? With huge figures being bandied about, more caps and mystery were in store.

Much of the controversy is due to the fact that the cap's history had not been adequately researched and documented. Auction houses and collections have tried to establish the cap's ownership and year of issue without having all of the sales records and all of the caps in collections available to them.

A year later another baggy green, this time reported to be Bradman's cap from his record-breaking first tour to Britain in 1930, went to auction at Christie's on 22 June 2004. This cap, undated and made by Harding's Mercery, was given by Bradman to a steward, Leonard Mills, on an Orient liner. The Australians travelled to and from England on the *Nairana*, and the catalogue states that the cap was undated. This is unusual: pre-1930 caps bore no date, but a Clarrie Grimmett cap sold in 1998 was clearly dated 1930.

Christie's claimed that Grimmett's cap, which was auctioned 13 May 1998, was specially manufactured for him, the inference being that the date had been added especially for Grimmett and did not appear on other 1930 caps. The 'Specially manufactured' mark on the label was printed on all 1930 caps, but in this situation it was taken to have a far more specific meaning.

The press has never questioned the lack of a date on the so-called Bradman cap, mainly because there has been no reference book produced that has collated information from museums, auction houses and official sources on the changes to baggy greens over the years. From 1928 to 1929 to 1932 to 1933 the cap underwent several changes in design, the inclusion of the date being the major one. Irrespective of the possible misdating of the cap, it was offered and sold as Bradman's 1930 baggy. The-then 21 year old performed brilliantly on that tour. The cap was sold for £35,850 (AU$93,790). Although this was less than the prices achieved pre-auction by Ludgrove's for the other caps – AU$200,000 and almost AU$500,000 – it was a significant amount.

Two other 1930 caps have been offered at auction: Ted a'Beckett's cap was offered at Leski Auctions in Melbourne on 13 December 2001 and Tim Wall's at Leski's on 28 June 2006; both bore the date '1930'. The Grimmett and Wall caps bore English cap maker's name Scholium.

To further explain the lack of a date on the 1930 Bradman cap, Christie's cited the donation of Bradman's 1928–29 cap to the State Library of South Australia seven months earlier, in November 2003. Bradman had given the cap to a neighbour, schoolboy Peter Dunham, in the 1950s. Christie's reasoned that if this cap, made by Harding's Mercery, was Bradman's then the cap made by Harding's going to auction, also undated and given by Bradman after 1930, must be from that tour. Bradman had played only two series up to that point. After 1930 caps were made by Farmer's of Sydney.

It is possible caps were made by two manufacturers for the same tour. David Studham from the Melbourne CC's library suggested this to me in late 2006. The date does not appear on Bradman's cap in any of the images from that tour that I have seen. The only photograph showing a dated cap is a studio shot with Bradman in cap and blazer. Possibly the players or Bradman used a new cap from Harding's on tour and the 1930 dated caps came later: either that, or Bradman chose to wear an earlier model.

With the market so buoyant it seemed inevitable that the 1946–47 cap given to Tim Biles and now owned by Cam Tingley would come on the market. In 30 September 2004 Michael Ludgrove, by then at Lawsons-Menzies, tried to sell it, with estimates of $300,000 to $500,000. While there were five pages of description there was no mention of the cap's manufacturer, the label or any owner's name. The cap was passed in. A year later the same auction house presented the cap again and it was sold for a reported $95,400.

In November 2004 the final Bradman cap to appear came on the market. Sensationally, it was another 1948. Imagine how Tim Serisier felt. When he bought his 1948 cap in July 2003, there was just one Invincibles cap and only six Bradman caps in existence. Eighteen months later there were nine caps and, most dramatically, two from his famous farewell series.

This final cap from 1948 was offered to the State Library of South Australia by Kevin Truscott. Bradman had given it to Kevin's father after the 1948 tour and it had remained within the family. The late Barry Gibbs, the-then manager of the Bradman collection, researched the circumstances of the dual caps and uncovered the existence of contracts specifying that the players were issued with two caps. It was on display in the library and its website; the cap, made by Farmer's, is marked in handwriting 'DG Bradman'.

The front page of Adelaide's *The Advertiser*, adorned with a colour photograph, proudly proclaimed: 'A gift to us. The Don's cap comes home'.[73] Given the vast sums achieved for Bradman caps and the bizarre twists and turns surrounding their marketing Kevin Truscott's donation was very generous, and it was fitting that the 1948 cap came home this way, as a donation, given that Sir Donald had given away his caps as gifts.

Other Bradman caps on public display at the Bradman Museum were originally donated. A New South Wales cap given by Bradman to the vendor was bought in 2002 for an undisclosed sum, while South Australian cap was given directly to the museum. Later in 2008 the Robbins 1948 cap bought by Tim Serisier was offered at Leski Auctions. The estimates were an eye-watering $600,000 to $700,000. It sold post auction for a reported $468,000, including premiums by a London-based Australian, Greg Coffey, and has been on display at the Sydney Cricket Ground Museum for much of the time since.

The effects of the GFC started to bite, especially with high-end sports collectables. In June 2011 Leski Auctions offered a 1934 cap that had not previously come to market, with estimates between $250,000 and $300,000. It was passed in twice during the year, the second time with the estimates lowered by $50,000.

In late 2012, incredibly, two Bradman caps were offered for sale. The Biles 1946–47 cap was offered by Ravenswick on 12 December 2012 with

No bids were received for Bradman's 1948 baggy green at Leski's auction house in 2008 and it was passed in, despite much pre-auction interest. (Newspix)

estimates between $120,000 and $180,000, but it was passed in. Three days later the 1934 was tried again with reduced estimates between $150,000 and $200,000 and it again failed to sell, as it had in May 2015. Finally, in December 2017, six and a half years after the first attempt, it was sold by Mossgreen Auctions in Melbourne for $148,800, inclusive of premiums.

Another well-known but never offered Bradman cap came to market in a blaze of publicity by Pickles Auctions in Adelaide: the undated Peter Dunham cap. The vendor had been convicted of fraud and the creditors hoped the cap would bring a sizeable return. Pre-market speculation spoke of it rivalling the $1,007,500 raised when Shane Warne's cap was auctioned for the Australian Red Cross bushfire appeal in January 2020. Interestingly, and a sign of the changing balance of power in world cricket,

The Dunham Bradman 1928–29 cap auctioned by Pickles in 2020. (Image courtesy of Michael Fahey)

the Bradman cap was described as the 'Taj Mahal of baggy greens'. Given the Warne cap proceeds went to a charitable cause, it was highly unlikely the Bradman cap would approach these dizzying estimates. It failed to reach the reserve at auction, stalling at $391,500, and was sold post auction for $450,000 plus premium. The buyer was Sydney businessman Peter Freedman.

A number of Bradman caps including his Bodyline cap of 1932–33 have never come to market, and their whereabouts are unknown.

MF

Steve Waugh tries on the millennium baggy green ahead of the Test against India in January 2000. The skullcap was a replica of that worn 100 years earlier. (Newspix)

CHAPTER 7

Variations and oddities

Over the years there have been numerous cricket caps produced for official and unofficial Australian representative teams, the production of which can be seen as an homage to the Test cap. Once the 1899 cap established the appropriate colour and emblem most other representative caps have been of a similar green, with the variations on the badge based on the common theme of the kangaroo and emu.

In 1913 a team organised by Edgar Mayne toured North America, an Australian representative XI but with no official patronage. The badge on the cap and blazer contained a kangaroo and emu in gold wire either side of a large 'A'.

The 1919 AIF team cap that belonged to Bert Oldfield resides at Lord's. Made in England by George Lewin & Co, it is dark blue and has a rising sun badge based on the Australian army insignia, as well as a crown with a scroll. The inscription is 'Australian Commonwealth Military Forces'. Oldfield's is one of three known; another is at the Melbourne Cricket Club (Melbourne CC) museum in Melbourne and the third with a private collector.

Arthur Mailey organised a private but officially sanctioned tour of Canada and the US in 1932. A cap and blazer were produced incorporating the kangaroo, emu and rising sun, which surrounded a large 'A' with 'Canadian American Tour 1932' in

Steve Waugh with the Australian Centenary of Federation cap at the SCG Museum in 2001. (Newspix)

the scroll. A blazer pocket was auctioned at Ludgrove's and a cap is now on display at the Melbourne CC museum. On this tour the capped players wore their Australian caps, while those who were not Australian players wore the tour cap. This appears to have been based upon the 1912 cap.

A blazer that belonged to Bodyline umpire George Hele contained the cricket coat of arms but the two panels that normally have a white background are yellow.[74] It seems this was the only time the colours of the coat of arms were varied, a reasonable decision to differentiate between a player's and umpire's attire.

The Australian War Memorial (AWM) in Canberra has a photograph of a cricket team in a prisoner of war camp in Germany in 1943 with the players wearing homemade baggy green caps. This is a poignant reminder that the cap is a unifying national symbol.[75]

The July 2003 Ludgrove's catalogue contained the image of an unusual baggy green. Lot #318, from the Keith Johnson collection, was described as a 'Baggy Green Test cap, green wool, coat of arms worked in gold wire and coloured thread with early motto "Advance Australia". Foster of London maker's label, possibly commissioned by Keith Johnson for the 1945 services match.' This would appear to be incorrect, as a services blazer that was auctioned by Mullock Madeley in 2001[76] contained the Australian coat of arms and state badges with 'Victory Tests, England India, 1945' embroidered below.

Brenton Siggs, who produced a signed bat commemorating the Victory Tests, met many of the players and never saw a cap. He was unsure if one was produced and suggested that maybe each wore their particular service headgear; for instance, Keith Miller's RAAF XI cap, which is now on display at the AWM.

The 1960 Australian 2nd XI blazer featured three stumps in white with bats either side and a red ball on top. The word 'Australia' was in the scroll and 1960 below that.[77]

In 1967 an Australian representative team visited New Zealand for a 10-match tour. They played four matches against New Zealand, which were not accredited as Test matches. The cap was a traditional baggy green embroidered with 'NZ Tour 1967'. This was the first time the series opponents were listed on a cap rather than just the date of the series.

Various Australian rebel tours have used a cap. Possibly in deference to the baggy green, for legal reasons or to establish a separate identity, these were yellow rather than green. The Kerry Packer–funded World Series Cricket (WSC) caps were yellow – sometimes described as wattle gold – with the WSC logo: three stumps and ball. They also follow a slimmer, more English style. This was again a counterpoint to the establishment Australian cap. For the inaugural 1977–78 season the badge was directly embroidered, but from the following summer it was sewn on.

Kerry Packer's million-dollar Australian World Series Cricket Australian team of 1977-78, in yellow caps at Moorabbin Oval in Melbourne. (Newspix)

The caps for the rebel tours to South Africa from 1985 to 1987 were also predominantly gold. Best described as a golf hat, it had panels of different material and contained the logo of a kangaroo and springbok on a red cricket ball.

Initially seen as a threat to traditional cricket, the helmet is here to stay: the use of a helmet is now compulsory in Australia for every child batting in organised cricket and for wicket-keepers when standing up to the stumps. Players rarely if ever bat in a cap during a Test match, so the helmet is almost the extension of the cap: a 21st-century baggy green. There is some evidence to support this.

When Cricket Australia registered their brands in 2002–03 their new logo was included on all marketing paraphernalia, reports and websites and on the players' apparel. The new logo now adorns the player's Test and One Day International (ODI) shirts and is on their fielding hats and the ODI cap. Like the Test cap, the green Test helmet retained the cricket coat of arms. Further strengthening this re-evaluation of the Test helmet is the fact that the yellow ODI variation was phased out in 2002. Now players wear the green helmet in both forms of the game.

Michael Slater, famous for kissing his helmet when he scored a century on his first appearance at Lord's, explained the differing affections for cap and helmet and foreshadowed the possible inclusion of the helmet as a modern equivalent to the cap: 'I suppose it would have been a better feeling to have kissed the cap at Lord's but I kissed the badge and it's the same on both.'[78]

The helmet is a work in progress. With the introduction of protective gear it was initially a motorcycle helmet, but much tinkering has occurred over the years to improve the helmet's comfort and durability. The early helmets were heavy and hot and regularly made communication difficult. Albion continued researching and produced a more comfortable variation in 2003, the lighter one-piece, injection-moulded, plastic model first used by Michael Bevan. This helmet lost the embroidered badge and had a pad print of the coat of arms.

Acceptance of this helmet was slow, as the players complained they had not been consulted in the design process. This harks back to the players' long-held sense of ownership of the cap and badge and its design. A new generation of helmet, a combination of technology and heritage, was soon released, and the coat of arms featured prominently on it.

Australia won the New Year's Test against India in 2000 by an innings and 141 runs. The leading run scorers, Ricky Ponting 141 and Justin Langer 223, both with their Millennium caps at the presentation. (Newspix)

Shane Warne acknowledges the crowd by taking a bow at Melbourne Cricket Ground in December 2001. He typically wore a white floppy in the field, which was ironic given his later mega baggy green cap bushfire auction. (Newspix)

No Australian Test captain was more intrinsically linked to the baggy green than Steve Waugh. (Newspix)

Steve Waugh with his baggy green cap and lucky red rag during a photo shoot in Sydney in November 2003. (Newspix)

This cap was produced as a prototype by Albion and intended to commemorate the first Australia versus Bangladesh Test match, in 2003. The cap was manufactured with the striped material used to construct the Australian Test team blazer. (Image courtesy of Australian Gallery of Sport and Olympic Museum)

Batsman Michael Clarke examines his newly acquired baggy green ahead of his debut innings in the first Test of the India versus Australia series in Bangalore in October 2004. (Newspix)

A 2009 newspaper close portrait of Ricky Ponting, with his baggy green 'in need of repair', a similar predicament for Steve Waugh's cap late in his career. (Newspix)

A rare occurrence: three debutants in one match! Marcus North (left), Phillip Hughes (centre) and Ben Hilfenhaus all wear their new caps at the Wanderer's Ground in Johannesburg ahead of the first Test versus South Africa in 2009. (Newspix)

**PHILLIP HUGHES
1988-2014**

Macksville-born Phillip Hughes became the youngest man to score a century in a Sheffield Shield final when he posted 116 at the SCG during NSW's win against Victoria in 2007–08.

The dashing and unorthodox left-hand batsman had earned his first NSW cap earlier that season, aged just 18.

Hughes made three more first-class centuries at the SCG, having quickly become a crowd favourite.

The Phillip Hughes plaque mounted on the Australian team's dressing room balcony wall at the Sydney Cricket Ground. Hughes tragically died in November 2014 after being struck while batting for South Australia against New South Wales. (Newspix)

Matthew Hayden celebrates scoring the then highest Test score of all time during the Australia versus Zimbabwe series at the WACA in October 2003. (Newspix)

Waugh in 2002 at Albion's factory when his beloved baggy green was repaired. He met with Albion's general manager Ross Barrat and master cap maker Clemente Izurieta. (Image courtesy of Albion C&D)

With insurance and occupational health and safety issues so prevalent, helmet wear will almost certainly increase. With skin cancer concerns also growing, wide-brimmed sunhats might also become compulsory. Many cricket clubs now issue these sunhats as official kit to children's teams rather than traditional cricket caps. In a few years it is possible that the cap will be seen as anachronistic, similar to belts and buckles from 19th-century cricket.

This would not be the case if more players carried as deep a sense of the cap's history as Justin Langer. Batting against the Indians in Sydney in January 2000, Langer put aside his helmet and called for his 1900 replica cap when he was nearing his century. He kissed the badge and went on to score 223, although he had his tin hat on when he passed the 200 mark. It was the same for Steve Waugh, who rarely batted in his cap but had it on against Pakistan in Sharjah in 2002. On a placid pitch against a dual-spin attack he had the opportunity to achieve a rare feat. With last partner Glenn McGrath watching from the other end, Waugh advanced from 83 to 103 in an over. 'Scoring a hundred with a six and the baggy green on top of your head – it doesn't come much better than that,' he said.[79]

Will collectors unable to afford the increasingly expensive caps turn their attention to the only other piece of headwear carrying the relic from a different era – the helmet with the cricket coat of arms – or will they begin to collect the various ODI caps, the first of which was a baggy yellow? Perhaps they'll collect the baggy greens worn by Australia's highly successful women cricketers.

There have been a few recent additions to the saga of the now highly valued baggy green. The celebrated repair of Steve Waugh's battered old cap resulted in a peak-shaped piece being removed. What to do with a piece of one of Australia's most celebrated caps?

Ricky Ponting's baggy green cap is returned to its maker, Albion, in Sydney for repairs in January 2010. Master seamstress Myuong Park restored the cap in 45 minutes. (Fairfax)

The Steve Waugh Foundation, an organisation that assists children and young adults with rare diseases, in 2005 planned to offer 11 positions as foundation patrons; all would be members of the Steve Waugh Foundation First XI. It was decided to reward those patrons, each of whom was contributing $250,000, with something symbolic of Waugh's career and commitment to the cause. A piece of the cap's old cloth was mounted on the blades of 11 bats that he had used in a first-class match. Each bat was then framed with photographic tributes and a handwritten message of gratitude from Waugh. The result is an interesting sidelight to the baggy green story.

In 2010 the state of Ricky Ponting's dishevelled cap bore some criticism in the press. However, unbeknown to the journalist, two days earlier

Albion supplied a bag to Test players to protect their baggy greens. This is Glenn McGrath's, photographed in 2004 a few days before his 100th Test. (Newspix)

Ponting had given his cap to Albion for a makeover as it was falling apart at the seams and he feared the peak would fall off.

After Albion Hat & Cap Co repaired and cleaned Steve Waugh's cap, national sales manager Ross Barrat realised that the years of beer and sweat were taking a toll on the fabric. With more players wearing the one cap for 100 or more Tests, the baggy greens were being loved to death. Subsequent steam clean jobs for the caps of Adam Gilchrist and Justin Langer confirmed Barrat's fears.

Barrat thought of a way to protect the caps from dirty gear, boots and spills. The result, now given as a gift from the company to each player, is a bag made from green cotton embroidered with the cricket coat of arms, the player's name and his Test number. Steve Waugh was given the first bag, followed by Gilchrist and Langer. It was first presented only to those whose caps needed attention but is now being done for all players, many of whom hang the cap bags on their locker door in the Australian dressing room. Other countries who buy their caps from Albion have adopted this practice.

Shane Warne (left), Justin Langer (right) and Glenn McGrath, who had just played their last Test matches, celebrate defeating England in the fifth Ashes Test match at the SCG. (Alamy)

In 2000, 160 Test players gathered in Sydney for an inaugural reunion, one open to every former Australian Test cricketer. This event was inspired by Allan Border and Greg Matthews and also included the naming of the team of the century. With Test numbers being introduced on players' shirts for the 2001–02 series, the reunion presented an opportunity to present all past players with a record of their chronological Test number. In July 2003 the Australian Cricket Board (ACB) and the Australian Cricketers' Association held a dinner in Sydney, and 147 of the 197 living Test players attended. Another 15 attended via video link from London.

Albion made a two thirds–sized miniature cap that was presented to each player. The cap contained a scaled-down embroidered coat of arms, and the ACB had each cap boxed with a glass top and an engraved plaque. Interestingly, a number of former players have asked Albion to embroider their Test number onto the back of their miniature cap.

Steve Waugh (left), Warne (middle) and McGrath at the 2001 Wimbledon tennis championship cheering on Patrick Rafter. (Alamy)

The traditions and legacy of the baggy green continue to evolve, and the richness of its history deepens. The most curious baggy green variation, and possibly this definition stretches the meaning of the word, is a number of blue Oakley baseball-style caps. Harking back to the Wimbledon final that Nasser Hussain bemoaned in Chapter 3, the choice of caps worn and not worn made the newspapers again in January 2023. Not only did Steve Waugh wear his baggy green to the 2001 final between Australian

Australian Youth XI caps over the years. (Image courtesy of Craig Hawkins Collection)

Pat Rafter and Croatia's Goran Ivanišević, but apparently in the post-Test celebrations the day before there was talk of the whole team wearing the cap to the tennis. Famously reluctant cap wearers Shane Warne and Mark Waugh unsurprisingly didn't wear the cap to Wimbledon.

Another player who didn't refuse to wear the cap but didn't wear the cap on the day nevertheless was Damien Fleming. *The Times* of India on

18 January 2023 and sen.com.au both reported that Fleming admitted Warne, Mark Waugh and himself were the only three not wearing the baggy green cap. Fleming thought it had been the alcohol talking the night before when the concept was raised. Fleming said he was simply naïve not to wear the cap and got branded as a rebel alongside Warne and Waugh. Fleming advised, 'Nah, surely we're not [going to wear them]. I paid for it though.' Tongue in cheek, Fleming suggested it cost him his Test career, but his thoughts in 2023 provided some interesting insight.

Both Victorians, Warne and Fleming wore navy blue Oakley caps, possibly further inflaming the rebel squad perception. Fleming concluded: 'Tugga, if I knew it was going to have that sort of ramification I would have worn the baggy green. End of career. Harsh. And Patty [Rafter] lost.'

Steve Waugh's Forever Green presentation bat, one of just 11 of Waugh's match-used bats that were framed and contained a swatch of his baggy green cap. (Image courtesy of Michael Fahey)

MF

Brad Haddin in full Australia-branded VB training cap and shirt during a training session in Queensland in 2008 prior to leaving for the West Indies. (Newspix)

CHAPTER 8

Haddin's VB cap and the birth of Cricket Australia's cap

In May 2008 an event occurred that led to a major change in the awarding of the Australian cap. Today, only Test players are given the baggy green, and uncapped players – that is, non-Test players – wear a Cricket Australia (CA) logo–adorned cap if playing for an Australian XI in a tour match. This is a departure from more than 140 years of touring protocol. From the beginning of Australian tours overseas all members received the same kit irrespective of their Test status and irrespective of their chance of playing a Test.

Commentators now erroneously state, 'Just 466 players have worn the baggy green.' As of late 2023 Matthew Kuhnemann was the most recent Test debutant and is listed as number 466. Notwithstanding that the cap has not always been baggy nor green, the sentiment they are expressing is that only the 466 Test players have worn the cap but this is wrong: every touring player wore the cap we now call the 'Test cap'. Irrespective of whether or not they had played a Test, Australian players wore the Australian cricket cap when playing for an Australian XI on tour: that is, in an official tour match.

Numerous Ashes squads contained players who had not yet played a Test, and a number had the misfortune of not playing Test cricket at all. A quick scan reveals those from the 20th century and into the 21st century who made an Ashes tour wore the baggy green but never played Test cricket. For example: Ashley Noffke and Wade Seccombe in 2001; Wayne Holdsworth 1993; Ray Phillips 1985; Jack Potter 1964; Ian Quick 1961; Charlie Walker 1930 and 1938; John Ellis 1926; Sam Everett 1926; Harold Webster 1912; and Philip Newland 1905. While this is not a huge number, there will be others who toured the other Test-playing countries. As well, it doesn't account for those who toured but at the time had not yet played a Test.

The point is that all the squad players, whether in a tour match or Test, played in the same cap. The number of tour matches on many tours was substantial; the 1948 Invincibles were famously undefeated in the five Tests played, and they played another 26 first-class matches as well as three non–first-class games all wearing baggy green caps. However, the rise of One Day Internationals and now T20 competitions both national and franchise has almost meant the death of pre-Test tour games, but what event caused a change to cap policy?

On the 2008 tour of the West Indies, Brad Haddin was about to make his debut in the first Test of the series due to start on 22 May and, as is still the case, there would be a cap presentation ceremony before that game. One hurdle, in Haddin's mind at least, was the tour match, Jamaica Select XI versus the Australians at the Trelawny multipurpose stadium from 16 to 18 May was scheduled six days before the Test. The dilemma became: how could he wear the Australian cap in the tour game as he had done on previous tours but then be presented with the same cap the morning of the Test?

He didn't wear the baggy green in the tour game, but what he did wear caused a ruckus in Australia that reverberated across the UK. Such was the confusion, outrage and compromise that Haddin ended up wearing four different caps or hats on four consecutive playing days of cricket, the fourth day being the beginning of the Test match. On the first day, not wishing to keep in a white floppy hat, Haddin decided to wear the team's training cap: a baseball-style cap with a logo from sponsors VB on the front and Adidas to the rear. Wishing to express solidarity through clothing uniformity, the team followed suit and Australia fielded in the blue VB caps.

Australian media was ablaze the next three days. One report was headed: 'Former Players slam CA for selling the baggy green'. Believing it was a commercial ploy, dial-a-comment suspects were sought by the press for a provocative headline. Greg Matthews lashed out at CA in the *Herald Sun*: 'Money talks, you're selling your pride, selling the baggy green. It is a cheap thing.' Keith Stackpole was disappointed: 'There are certain things that should be sacred. You are representing Australia, not VB.'

CA public affairs manager Philip Pope advised the decision was not commercial but that the team had wanted uniformity in appearance. He further explained that Haddin was the only player in the team yet to receive a baggy green or play a Test. Matthews countered that every player chosen to tour should be entitled to a baggy green. Both made valid points, but it appeared the adoption of a new tradition once again had unintended consequences. Former players reared on the protocol that everyone gets a baggy green could only assume the adoption of the sponsor's cap was a commercial ploy. The players of the day, entranced by the power of the baggy green, wanted to respect the awarding of the cap but still present a unified group with team headware.

Stung by the criticism, the team responded on the second day by reverting to their baggy green caps as reported in *The Sydney Morning Herald* on 19 May. The report advised that the decision taken by team management on day one was to save wicket-keeper Brad Haddin from wearing a wide-brimmed hat. Management explained: 'As a mark of respect for the tradition of the baggy green, Haddin, who will become Australia's 400th [Test] player when he makes his debut against the West Indies on Thursday, would not yet wear one.' They then made the statement: 'Uncapped players usually wear a white hat during tour matches. But the wicket-keeper has rarely worn a white hat, so team management decided all players would instead wear the training caps. The team switched to their baggy greens on day two, while Haddin wore a white hat.'

Australia batted most of day two with Jamaica 0/11 from just five overs at close of play, so presumably Haddin kept in an unfamiliar white hat for just five overs.

On 20 May sports writer Spiro Zavos on The Roar website lashed the team. The headline was 'The Iconic blue VB and Adidas cap? I think not?' Spiro wrote: 'It was a disgraceful breach of tradition and an insult to the iconic baggy green cap for the Australian side in the West Indies to take the field in the opening first-class match of the tour wearing a blue cap.' He then made a further claim: 'Perhaps even more disgraceful than the assault on one of Australian cricket's greatest tradition was the explanation given by the team management for the obvious marketing ploy.'

Zavos advised Haddin should have worn the white floppy, which he acknowledged he did on day two. Matthews was quoted again claiming CA was 'selling out the baggy green cap', and Neil Harvey made the point: 'If they can't wear the Australian cap when playing for Australia, they shouldn't wear anything [possibly referring to his era of the 1950s, when bare heads were more common].'

The English, especially the players who were brow beaten by the cult of the baggy green in the late 1990s and early 2000s, saw a chance to pile-on. Michael Atherton writing in *The Times* under the heading 'England take historical high ground' on 22 May recounted his attempt to swap his England cap – 'one of those horrible Casey Jones creations' – for a baggy green at the end of the 1990–91 series. 'The contemptuous look that the Australian player concerned gave me was matched only by the incredulity on his part that I should think of such a thing.'

He then commented: 'Since then, I have always slightly shuddered at the memory whenever the cult of the baggy green has been rammed down English cricket's throat – which has been often. Justifiable pride, though, often morphed into syrupy self-parody: remember the puke-worthy sight of the Australia team cheering on Mark Philippoussis [sic] at Wimbledon wearing their baggy greens en-masse? Thankfully, the sermonising can stop. Last week, on the opening match of their tour to the West Indies against a Jamaica Select XI, Australia took to the field not only in garish baseball-style training caps, but ones bedecked with a sponsor's logo.'

(The tennis match was the 2001 five-set final and was actually between Australian Pat Rafter and eventual winner Goran Ivanišević. This baggy green–wearing event had reverberation that echoed some 15 years later. By the way, Mark Philippoussis was runner-up at Wimbledon in 2003, a non–Ashes Tour year.)

After the Haddin affair Cricket Australia created a cap for non-Test players selected for Australia in tour games. (Image courtesy of Michael Fahey)

In a considered article, *The Times*' sporting correspondent Kevin Eason summed up much that had appeared in the press but acknowledged Haddin's dilemma and noted the explanation by management that the training caps were used out of respect for the baggy green. Eason then reported they had come up with a compromise: make yet another hat. He quoted the CA statement: 'Cricket Australia has accepted that in future a "fitted green" cap may need to be developed so that players who have not yet represented Australia in [Test] cricket may wear an appropriate green felt cap.' Hats off to CA if that is allowed, he concluded.

It would appear the baggy green worn over the years by all Australian players would now solely be the domain of Test representatives.

Geoff McClure in *The Age* made the point that each day Haddin wore new headgear. For the final day, when he was again wicket-keeping, he chose to wear another cap – but not the green baggy as his teammates were wearing but rather his yellow ODI cap. McClure wondered how all this had happened, advising that in 2001 Steve Waugh and team manager Steve Bernard decided the cap would only be presented to those chosen in a Test XI.

In June 2008 *The Age* revisited the incident and discovered an image of Haddin wearing a baggy green for his tour match in 2001. He was sent to India as a replacement for the injured Adam Gilchrist and played against the Indian Board President's XI. CA was contacted and explained that later in 2001 on the Ashes tour skipper Steve Waugh and manager Steve Bernard ruled that the baggy green had taken on an aura, and that in future only Test XI players would be allowed to wear it. This meant that tourists such as Haddin, in India before the Ashes, and Ashley Noffke, the last non-Test player to wear one in England that year, would be deemed ineligible.

Interestingly, though, a search of images shows Haddin wearing a green cap again, this time in the tour match against Worcestershire in 2005. Was this 2001 edict enforced or was Haddin a serial offender?

There were numerous tours post Ashes 2001 and before the May 2008 incident; a few had tour games included. Finding a tour game where a non-Test player played is difficult, and where photos exist of that player even harder. One such event, however, is Jimmy Maher of Australia in action wicket-keeping during day one of the three-day tour match between the University of West Indies Vice Chancellor's XI on 26 April 2003 at the University of the West Indies cricket ground in Bridgetown, Barbados. He is keeping in what appears to be quite an old baggy green.

The Sydney Morning Herald reported on the game on 29 April 2003 under the banner 'Maher enjoys the chance to wear a different hat or two': 'Explaining afterwards that he had not received his own coveted baggy green cap as this was not a Test, Maher, 29, joked he had felt some of Matthew Hayden's magic anoint his head after using his headgear for the match. "I had to borrow one. That's Haydos's and that's probably why I got a hundred," he said. "When you play Tests, that's when you earn the baggy green cap and that's something I'm still trying to do."'

A fringe member of Australia's one-day team, Maher also borrowed the gloves of another player for the three-day tour game at the Three Ws Oval, giving wicket-keeper Adam Gilchrist a well-earned rest. Whether or not an edict was in place, at least for this tour of the West Indies, non-Test players were not given a baggy green but I guess nothing stops someone lending you theirs!

The upshot of the Haddin VB cap incident was that uncapped players are offered a CA cap with a kangaroo and emu supporting the CA logo, which is a shield with the sun casting a shadow of three stumps and the Southern Cross. This CA cap is the template for all other Australian teams

Long-time Australian wicketkeeper Brad Haddin. (Alamy)

such as Australia A, Australia under-19s and Australian Country XI, with the only difference being the wording embroidered below the crest.

More importantly, by virtue of the 2001 edict the Australian cap is now solely presented to Test players, and due to the 2008 incident CA logo caps are available for non-Test players.

MF

Ellyse Perry celebrates an Ashes Test match win in 2011 at Bankstown with oval cap in hand. (Newspix)

CHAPTER 9

Hats off to the women

The thrilling and irrevocable rise of women's cricket at the start of the 21st century prompted a re-evaluation of the Australian game and its time-honoured symbol, the baggy green cap. No longer was the women's game seen as an adjunct to the men's game. With extraordinary strength and resilience it had established its own unbreakable identity, and its elite players exercised their right to wear the same cap as their male counterparts.

To the cognoscenti this was unsurprising, given women and girls had played with varying degrees of skill and flair since well before the formation of the Australian Women's Cricket Council in 1931–32. Furthermore, Australia had been a foundation member of the International Women's Cricket Council (IWCC) in 1958. As in every other facet of society the women's gains were hard won over generations, and after a final two years of intense negotiations Women's Cricket Australia (WCA) and the Australian Cricket Board (ACB) integrated in 2003 to be rebadged as Cricket Australia (CA), the game's supreme administrative body.

By 2017 the 'Southern Stars', the sobriquet for the national women's team, was finally scrapped, and like the men the elite XI could bestride the world stage without a nickname. They were simply and proudly the Australian women's cricket team.

That a crowd of 86,174 attended the mighty Melbourne Cricket Ground in March 2020 to see the team conquer India and win their sixth and third consecutive Twenty20 World Cup was testament to their relevance and status in Australian and world sport.

For Belinda Clark, the unrivalled batter and visionary administrator immortalised in a bronze statue at the Sydney Cricket Ground, it was the fulfilment of a daring and, for so long, a seemingly impossible dream. A mentor and inspiration to a generation of young girls and boys, in 2003 Clark was the first Australian women's cricket captain to wear the baggy green with the distinctive cricket coat of arms – which, in one form or another, had been the custom for elite male players since 1899.

That little or no thought was given to the headwear for Australia's elite female players throughout the 20th century was symptomatic of the indifference shown to the rights and needs of the women's game. While in the 1990s and early 2000s Mark Taylor and Steve Waugh enacted rituals to guarantee the sanctity of the baggy green cap, elite women players still grappled with headbands and dodgy baseball and merchandise caps with hand-embroidered logos, Commonwealth coat of arms stitched in various sizes and inelegant bucket, and flannelette or floppy canvas and beret-styled hats.

The Australian women coming out to field when they met the women of Kent in a one-day match at Sevenoaks, Kent on 19 May 1951. Not a cap of any sort in sight. (Alamy)

Joanne Broadbent in her Commonwealth coat of arms cap at the nets in the UK in 1998. (Alamy)

Ann Mitchell, a renowned administrator who managed Australian teams and served as president of the IWCC from 1982 to 1988, has vivid memories of visiting the headquarters of Albion Sports to collect not baggy green caps but broad-brimmed sunhats endorsed by Greg Chappell. In essence, however, the leading women players from the 1970s, much like their pioneering predecessors from first Test captain Margaret Peden in 1934, were more concerned about the marginalisation of the women's game, the paucity of matches organised and the lack of opportunities available to girls.

Clark said: 'Rather than symbols it was more a matter of an earnest desire to play more.' Clark was a pre-eminent figure in international women's cricket who served as chief executive officer of WCA and then in senior positions with Cricket Australia after captaining Australia in the three forms of the game from 1993–94 to 2005.

Christina Matthews, a fine wicket-keeper who made her debut seven years earlier than Clark in a green cap with a sewn-on patch of a style found in souvenir shops, agreed there were greater issues confronting the women's game. 'In those days we were just so happy that we were allowed to play as so little women's cricket was played. And going on a tour was just like gold.'

Australian captain Belinda Clark examines her cap in 2001 prior to touring England. (Newspix)

After her record 20-Test career, Matthews served WCA and Cricket New South Wales as an administrator before being appointed chief executive officer of the Western Australian Cricket Association in 2011. 'Certainly, there was no sense of depravation because it had taken us so long to get a cap of any description,' Matthews added. She played her entire career under the commonwealth's and not cricket's coat of arms.

Growing up in country New South Wales, Alex Blackwell, who like Clark captained Australia in the three forms of the game, was oblivious to the existence of the women's cap, let alone a competition where it could be attained. However, by the time she progressed through the ranks and made her international debut during 2002, two events in 1997 had significantly changed the complexion of Australian women's cricket and the public perception of it.

Delighted Australia had overpowered New Zealand in Calcutta to win the fourth of a possible six world cups in 24 years, a more enlightened ACB executive invited Clark and her triumphant team to pause their return journey in Sydney and undertake a lap of honour on the first day of the men's New Year Test between Australia and South Africa. To Clark, this was the first overt show of support for the women's team by the ACB, which in the spirit of greater understanding and perhaps contrition also extended the invitation to the players' families. It was a dizzying experience for the team, which had mostly paid their way to the tournament and was further heightened when South African captain Hansie Cronje made a point of leaving the dressing room to congratulate and shake the hand of each player.

At about the same time, emerging Victorian batter Mel Jones wrote to WCA chief executive Sue Crow lamenting the fact that Australia's finest women cricketers wore dodgy baseball caps while the men continually added lustre to the legend of the baggy green. To both Clark and Matthews it was a defining moment: the first time the cap was formally placed on the agenda at WCA as the winds of change gathered strength.

'I felt strongly about it as I grew up reading and hearing so much about the baggy green and the significance the boys attached to it,' Jones said. 'I believed the same respect should be accorded the women but I was unsure about writing and talked it over with my mother, Marie, who said if I felt that strongly I should act. So I did,' Jones added. She scored a Test century and played 61 one-day matches before serving as a CA board member and working as a commentator on both the women's and men's games.

Soon after integration, Clark and her team were issued with a baggy green cap identical to that worn by the men but for the reversal of the scroll colours, with 'Australia' embroidered in red on a gold background. While Jones believed the subtle variation can prompt worthwhile discussion about the distinctly different histories of the women's and men's caps, Blackwell, a leading advocate for women and LGBTQI people in sport, holds a contrary view. 'I think the women's cap should be the same as the men's,' she said on many occasions. 'I didn't see the reversing of the ribbon as a positive. I think it implied separation, not unity. I think it says you can have it but it is not the real one.

'That said, I applaud Cricket Australia for the alignment and the retrospective presentation of the caps. This was a lovely recognition for all those who had played.'

Tina Macpherson, a fast bowler who played one Test match and took the first five-wicket haul for Australia at the inaugural world cup in England in 1973, is representative of the scores of women who sacrificed so much to play the game when it was unfashionable to do so and players met their own costs. 'My baggy green is my pride and joy,' Macpherson said, eyes sparkling. 'It means so much to me and I am so proud.'

A senior citizen who has long volunteered at the Bradman Museum and International Cricket Hall of Fame at Bowral, Macpherson has spoken to service clubs about her pride in the cap and the joy of playing in the world cup, which predated by two years the first world cup for men. 'Can you imagine a girl from Cowra who started playing at [age] 13 and was only allowed to field for men's teams bowling at Lord's and being presented to Princess Anne. Can you imagine? In my day a baggy green cap equated to a "pretty good cricketer" but it was not talked about much by the girls of the time. I had a canvas hat, something that could be folded to go with the culottes [that] were hardly turning heads,' she said with characteristic mischievousness.

In recording Macpherson's accomplishment in her world cup report for the 1974 *Wisden Cricketers' Almanack*, noted English cricketer, writer and administrator Netta Rheinberg could not resist a nod to history on behalf of the women's game: 'In 1777 the Third Duke of Dorset watched the Countess of Derby's XI play a Ladies' Invitation team at The Oaks in Surrey. He wrote afterwards: "What is human life but a game of cricket? And if so, why should not the ladies play it as well as we?"'

The first recorded women's cricket match in Australia was at Sandhurst, now Bendigo, in Victoria in 1874 and was a light-hearted contest won by 21 runs by the Blues over the Reds.

Historically, Australia's women cricketers met their privations and impoverishment with good humour and camaraderie and cheekily recognised the baggy green presented fashion dilemmas only occasionally experienced in the men's dressing room. 'We used to joke among our peers just what we would do with our hair when every two years we would get the chance to wear the baggy green,' Blackwell said, pointedly alluding to the ever-diminishing number of Test matches being organised in the wake of multi-format series. 'What to do with bun or pony: park it or roll it?'

Some players were more suited to the cap than others and some discarded it after the first session of play. Certainly this was so of Clark and Lisa Keightley, who, like Shane Warne and Mark Waugh, invariably opted for broad-brim cover. For all its significance, Clark and Blackwell note the cap is not the most practical headwear as it fails to offer the required protection from the sun. 'From that perspective it is not very practical at all,' Clark said.

For Blackwell, whose identical twin Kate also played for Australia, any required wearing of a cap conflicted with family values that emphasised the protection of the head from both the sun and short-pitch bowling. From the age of 11, the twins' mother insisted they bat in helmets – navy and white for the benefit of the scorers – after Alex was struck on the cheekbone in a game against a boys' team.

Ellyse Perry is presented with her Test cap by former Australian wicket-keeper Christina Matthews at the Australia versus England Women's Ashes Test at Bradman Oval at Bowral in 2008. (Newspix)

Alex Blackwell (centre) celebrates a 2011 Ashes Test win with Rene Farrell and Sarah Elliott wearing the women's baggy green. (Newspix)

As an adolescent she may have been oblivious to much of the romancing of the baggy green, but Blackwell certainly understands the mystique surrounding the shape of a baggy cap. She fell under its spell while wearing one of green, yellow and navy for the Serviceman's Club at Griffith and a black one when representing Riverina High School. 'That was a little bit like wearing an oven on our head,' Blackwell mused.

Nowadays the women have a deep pride in the cap and, like the men, place great store in the presentations to debutants. Certainly Clark has a strong memory of welcoming Amanda-Jade Wellington into the fold the summer of 2017–18, the season that heralded the arrival of Beth Mooney to the Test match arena after a two-year acclimatisation in the short-form game. Such was her development that Mooney became a household name at a pace once reserved for the likes of Ellyse Perry, Alyssa Healy, the late Phillip Hughes and Patrick Cummins, and in 2020 and 2022 she was adjudged the leading woman cricketer in the world by *Wisden Cricketers' Almanack*.

Perry, too, was similarly honoured in 2016 and 2019 when named alongside Cummins as one of *Wisden*'s five cricketers of the year, one of the most prestigious accolades in the game. Perry is the first woman to

Two First Nations Australian players, Jason Gillespie and Faith Thomas, at Adelaide Oval in 2016 wearing their caps. (Newspix)

have achieved this rare double, which has only been attained by three men: Kumar Sangakkara, Kane Williamson and Virat Kohli.

Mooney and Perry both served under Meg Lanning, *Wisden*'s first leading woman cricketer in the world in 2014 and the celebrated captain of the fabulous team that so enthralled the record crowd at the Melbourne Cricket Ground in 2020 as the women's game was finally enshrined in Australian sporting culture.

MC

The fate of his baggy green was the main talking point ahead of David Warner's farewell Test match over the summer of 2023-24. (Newspix)

CHAPTER 10

Capital appreciation

Since the mid-1990s intense public interest in the cultural and monetary significance of the baggy green has caused cap owners to experience a full range of emotions. Certainly there are a good number of Test cricketers and their descendants who regret they were so unsentimental about the cap. Baggy greens have been lost, sold, swapped, gifted, loaned, donated and neglected, as was David Warner's before his final Test match in 2024. Conversely, caps have been collected, bought, borrowed and, indeed, stolen. For some collectors and contemporary players they have become valuable objects insured for many thousands of dollars and kept under lock and key.

By the start of the 21st century the baggy green had become an object of desire that compelled owners to re-evaluate their relationship with what was once simply an item of national sporting dress. 'That there are so few of them is what makes them a very special piece,' Ian Redpath, the celebrated batsman and former Geelong antique dealer, said. 'They don't come out of captivity too often. They are very sought after and those who collect them are very genuine in their desire to have them. It's not like collecting Dinky toys. The baggy green is of national importance.'

Ian Redpath, seen here at the MCG in 1975, is well qualified to talk about the cap's significance. (Newspix)

For many years the cap could be replaced on request and often was. For some players the blazer had greater significance, while for others it was the short-sleeved jumper or simply the green and gold colours they held so dear. 'I must admit the baggy green was something to be worn just as a blazer was to be worn to go to lunch,' nonagenarian Neil Harvey said, the last survivor of the 1948 Invincibles.

Harvey said the word 'memorabilia' was not even in the dictionary when he was playing, and he rarely wore a cap at the crease or in the field. He gave away all his caps bar the Invincibles baggy green and blazer, which, along with the Don Bradman Sykes bat he used just once for his unforgettable 112 and 4 not out at Headingley in 1948, is in the proud possession of his daughter Anne.

Among others to receive a baggy green from Harvey were Simpson 'Sammy' Guillen, a member of the exclusive fraternity to have played Test cricket for two countries – West Indies and New Zealand – and St George rugby league hooker Ernest Harold 'Tiger' Black, who after serious injury served the game as an administrator and renowned broadcaster for commercial radio in Sydney.

By no means was Tiger Black the only prominent member of the media to benefit from the generosity of Australian players. Colin McDonald, who broadcast cricket for the ABC, gave one of his caps to Englishman Brian 'Johnners' Johnston, who was renowned for bringing a touch of vaudeville to his commentary. Following his death in 1994 the family auctioned the cap for charity. Keith Stackpole gave caps to Rex Pullen, a long-serving sports journalist at the-then *Herald Sun* organisation in Melbourne and to the family of Mike Williamson, well known in the southern states for his Australian Rules football commentary.

Celebrated opening batsman and much-loved raconteur Arthur Morris died aged 93 in 2015 without a baggy green in his possession. He gave one to Frank Worrell, the first black captain of the West Indies outside the Caribbean and a statesman among the game's leaders. Another beneficiary was a young Indian boy who made some runs while Morris was in Mumbai for a charity match.

While sympathetic to their predecessors who lost rather than gained money through their association with the game, the modern cricketer finds it difficult to accept the sale of a baggy green. 'I get a little distressed when I see a player selling it off for financial gain,' Steve Rixon observed.

'I just couldn't imagine selling it even in the most difficult times. Other things can be offered but not the cap. Let's keep that sacred.'

'You are never far enough in debt to sell an Australian cap,' Ross Edwards said. 'Never: no matter how much you'd get. Get rid of everything but not the cap. I'm a little ashamed that I swapped mine for a bobby's helmet. It's an iconic emblem. I'd be very surprised, indeed, disappointed, if this wasn't the view of all cricketers. I would have to think less of an Australian cricketer who did not appreciate the reverence of the baggy green. I would be very surprised if this is not a universal feeling.'

'When I hear of the auctions I don't think that it is crass commercialism, I think it is maybe unfortunate that they had to sell them,' paceman and pundit Geoff Lawson said with characteristic pragmatism. 'But if it was a contemporary player earning millions of dollars and selling a cap, I would be dirty about that.'

Certainly millions of dollars were not on offer when Terry James Jenner and Kerry James O'Keeffe, proud leg spinners who debuted two months apart against England in 1970–71, lost their way in mid-life. Jenner, who died in 2011 at the age of 66, spent 18 months in prison at the close of the 1980s after embezzling money from an employer to pay gambling debts. Renowned as coach and adviser to the peerless Shane Warne, 'TJ', as he was universally known, presented his first baggy green to his father Arthur soon after he played his final Test match against the West Indies in 1975. 'I'm glad my father had it when I really did it hard. There is no doubt I would have sold it and for very little too,' Jenner admitted.

Before his death at the age of 84 in 2002 Arthur returned the cap to Jenner, who bequeathed it to his daughter Trudianne along with his Australian sweater.

O'Keeffe, who brought his own language to the broadcasting of the game, described this period of his life as 'being in the driest of gullies'. Throughout the 1990s he worked at a string of temporary, unsuitable and modestly paid jobs and felt as dispirited as he was unfulfilled. O'Keeffe's first baggy green was still in his possession when he reached his driest of gullies and he is still haunted by the memory of selling it for $5,000 to a collector in country New South Wales.

'The dearest thing I had had to go to get me through a tough time,' O'Keeffe said with considerable emotion. 'It really hurt and nagged me that while I had not cheapened it I had seen a dollar value whereas I had never seen a dollar value on the cap. Not ever. Even though the players are wealthy now they still revere the cap and I had that reverence for it, but my situation affected my regard for it. I regretted it at the time but now must accept it and be thankful I still have a cap.'

Rodney Hogg said he should be locked up for swapping his cap for an English bobby's equipment. (Newspix)

That a baggy green has its own shelf in a walk-in robe at his home is the result of an act of great selflessness by the sons of one of O'Keeffe's cricketing pals, the late John McLaughlin. In the mid-1970s when O'Keefe despaired of regaining a place in the Australian team he was grateful for the constant support and reassurance of his friend, and it proved well founded when O'Keeffe was selected for the first Test against Pakistan at Adelaide in December 1976, almost three years since his previous appearance against New Zealand in Auckland.

O'Keeffe conceded he was tired and emotional at a Christmas function when he spontaneously presented McLaughlin with a baggy green. Since the death of their father, Peter and Mark McLaughlin had heard O'Keeffe during radio broadcasts lamenting the fact he did not have a cherished baggy green cap. The boys knew what their father would have expected of them, and in 2006 they honoured his memory by presenting O'Keeffe with the cap at the Kyle Bay Bowling Club. It was a magnanimous gesture that effectively completed O'Keeffe's rehabilitation to a normal life as Australia's 253 Test match cricketer.

If Ross Edwards felt ashamed about swapping a cap with a member of the English constabulary, he was not alone. Doug Walters, Jeff Thomson, Max Walker, Ashley Mallett, David Hookes and Alan Turner also confessed to such a bizarre transaction with a bobby. Such aberrant behaviour was not, however, confined to the early and mid-1970s. At the world cup in 1979 Rodney Hogg swapped a cap, not for a bobby's helmet but for the officer's lapel identification number, baton and handcuffs. 'I should lock myself up, shouldn't I?' Hogg conceded.

Thomson did not stop at a bobby's helmet. In the Caribbean in 1978 he traded a baggy green for the field medals belonging to a monolithic Jamaican policeman and Commonwealth Games athlete who had protected the Australians during the riots at Sabina Park in Kingston during the tour. 'He was a huge bloke who had taken a bullet or two in his time. Can't remember his name,' Thomson observed laconically.

Certainly there is an increasing need for past owners of the baggy green to be philosophical, perhaps even forgiving. Genial, undemanding Brian Booth, who died at the age of 89 in 2023, encapsulated it best when he observed: 'When you give the baggy green away it is really up to the recipient to do what they want with it.' Booth had a fond memory of a voice ringing out over the glorious Worcester ground on his first visit to England in 1961: 'When I got my first run I heard someone say: "Congratulations on your first run on English soil." It was [distinguished English batsman] Tom Graveney and I always held Tom in the highest regard,' Booth said.

Australian rugby league legend Johnny Raper and another famous hat. Raper was a recipient of the gift of a baggy green. (Newspix)

Although only directly opposed in three Test matches in 1962–63, they became good friends and Booth happily presented Graveney with a baggy green. In the early 2000s Booth learned it had been included in a sale of Graveney's cricket memorabilia, which is not an uncommon practice. Indeed, in March 2007 at the Nottingham racecourse the cap Arthur Morris swapped with England leg spinner Eric Hollies in 1950–51 fetched £3,600 at auction.

It is impossible to know how many baggy greens are in existence and their whereabouts. Many are either in the hands or have left the hands of the descendants of players, collectors and investors. For instance, it is documented that Australia's 25th Test captain, Ian Johnson, presented his cap to Stuart Surridge after Surrey beat the 1956 Australian team. Surridge died aged 74 in 1992. Just months after retiring from Test cricket in 2007 Justin Langer was given Keith Miller's 1956 baggy, which had been auctioned in Melbourne in 2006 two years after Miller's death at the age of 84. Allan Border provided a cap for rugby league champion Johnny Raper while Alan Davidson presented one to tennis ace Neale Fraser, who was given to wearing it at the crease for the Melbourne Cricket Club's Club XI.

Before they were required to sign a statutory declaration to replace it many players were given to swapping caps with an opponent, although Bob Simpson said it was a practice frowned upon by the game's governors. Be that as it may, Simpson has the caps of his great pal Ken Barrington (England), Fred Titmus (England) and Conrad Hunte (West Indies) from his first stint as Australian captain.

Allan Border, Steve Waugh and Dean Jones, who died aged 59 in 2020, managed to build impressive collections without surrendering the baggy greens of greatest importance to them. Border treasures his first cap, which he estimates he wore for the first 80 of his then record 156 Test matches, while Jones was particularly enamoured of the cap he donned for his career-defining 210 in the tied Test with India at Chennai in September 1986.

Border has caps worn by Allan Lamb and Wayne Larkins (England), Javed Miandad (Pakistan), Duleep Mendis (Sri Lanka), Paul McEwan (New Zealand), Kepler Wessels (South Africa), Jeff Dujon (West Indies) and Chetan Chauhan (India).

Waugh swapped with Neil Foster (England), Saeed Anwar (Pakistan), Mohammad Azharuddin (India), Hansie Cronje (South Africa) and Ravi

Ratnayeke (Sri Lanka). Jones swapped jumpers for caps worn by Javed Miandad, Viv Richards (West Indies), Martin Crowe (New Zealand) and Kapil Dev (India), while Max Walker, who died aged 67 in 2016, owned the caps of Derek Underwood (England), Andy Roberts (West Indies) and Dayle Hadlee (New Zealand), Kim Hughes has caps worn by Mike Brearley (England) and Viv Richards (West Indies), Graham McKenzie has the cap of England's Welsh fast bowler Jeff Jones and Jason Gillespie the cap of England paceman Darren Gough.

Perhaps inevitably, given its allure and mystique, the baggy green became the prey of the nefarious within the cricket community and beyond. Ricky Ponting, Michael Kasprowicz, Ian Healy and Gillespie each had a cap stolen as the commercial value of the artefact increased exponentially during the 1990s. Graham McKenzie, among others, had a cap purloined when less thought was given to its significance and worth. This did not, however, lessen the sense of loss or quell the anger at the time.

Seldom does the aggrieved player learn the identity of the culprit, and only a successful police investigation or admission of guilt and offer of restitution by the offender can provide some solace. On only very rare occasions is a player reunited with his cap. At Adelaide Oval in 2000 Cricket Australia executives ceremoniously presented to gallant and genial indigenous fast bowler Gillespie his baggy green, which was stolen during a tour of South Africa in 1997 and discovered at an auction two years later. 'I went through all my kit and it became really clear that it disappeared because I was quite anal about where I kept my baggy green,' Gillespie said. 'It went walkabout either at the ground or at the hotel – all I knew [was] that it was gone.

'It was just a relief, really, to have it back. I had a replacement but as soon as I got my original one back I reverted to that, the one I wore for the majority of my career. To have my original back was really nice. It's not just a cap, it's what it represents – the hard work and effort that's gone into reaching the stage of being presented a cap. Cherish it because it's your own personal achievement and the cap on your head symbolises that you've earned it.'

Ian Healy's cap was also recovered when by chance Mark Taylor found it showcased at a Sydney suburban cricket centre.

Gillespie's was not the first baggy green to be stolen in South Africa, as Australia's 34th captain Ian Chappell ruefully attests. In February 1970

Century makers Ian Healy (left) and Steve Waugh proudly wearing the baggy green amid a dressing room full of cricketing gear in Brisbane in 1998. (Newspix)

Chappell was trudging up the stairs to the dressing room at the bloodhouse that can be the Bullring at the Wanderers Stadium in Johannesburg, angry at being bowled for a duck by hard-nosed Eddie Barlow. A moment later he was seething when a spectator daringly snatched his cap. 'As I hit the stairs some bastard took it off the top of my head,' Chappell said, and from that moment forth he removed his cap as he made his way back to the pavilion.

However, as Chappell will explain when holding court, there is an amusing sequel to the tale of woe: 'Many years ago in Perth I went to dinner at the home of a mate, Simon Davis, who I met in Rhodesia [now Zimbabwe] at the start of the South African tour in 1966–67,' Chappell recounted. 'Another guy from Zimbabwe was there and he said: "I've got a cap of yours." I said: "You're not the bastard who it took it off my head?" And he replied: "No, but I might have bought it from the bloke who did!"'

While Chappell is steeped in the history of the game and has an intimate knowledge of it, he has no emotional attachment to the baggy green cap. In fact, he is troubled by what he considers the ostentatious displays of the cap that became increasingly fashionable during the first two decades of the 21st century. Like his brothers Greg and Trevor, he does not have one baggy green among his possessions and nor, he said, does he know the whereabouts of any of them.

It was not until 2005 when collaborating with former teammate and author Ashley Mallett for the successful book *Chappelli Speaks Out* (Allen & Unwin, 2007) that he learned one of his caps was conspicuously presented along with those donated by Greg Chappell and Graeme Hole in a showcase on a stairway at the Glenelg Cricket Club in Adelaide, where he launched his luminous career.

Coincidentally, Mallett, the laconic off spinner and gully specialist who died age 76 in 2021, had two caps stolen in extraordinary circumstances during his 38-Test career between 1968 and 1980. The extent to which someone will go to steal a baggy green was graphically illustrated to Mallett when he was 12th man at a major match for charity in 1974–75. On this occasion his duties extended beyond the dressing room and he moved among the spectators at the Melbourne Cricket Ground to collect donations for the victims of Cyclone Tracy, which had devastated Darwin on Christmas Day 1974 and claimed 50 lives on land and 16 at sea. As he rattled the tin for the cause a villain in a group that had surrounded him deftly removed the cap from his hip pocket and disappeared into the mob. Mallett knew nothing of its fate or whether it ever reached the memorabilia market in Australia or England.

However, an extraordinary letter from a member of the English establishment in November 1998 provided the definitive explanation for the disappearance of his England tour cap stolen from the Marylebone Cricket Club (Marylebone CC) members' changing room at Lord's in 1972. Richard Robins, the godson of Don Bradman and a recipient of a baggy green from the game's greatest batsman, confessed to nicking Mallett's cap after a pre-season practice session with his mates at the Nursery Ground at Lord's.

Ashley Mallett's 1979–80 baggy green, which came with a handwritten authentication from Ashley. (Image courtesy of Michael Fahey)

Robins wrote: 'In 1972 when you toured with the Australian side, your team used the Members' changing room in which to leave all their kit and I am afraid that many of us young [Marylebone CC] players used to try on the baggy green caps [that] were lying around the changing area. I tried yours on and it fitted extremely well. To my great shame I kept it (leaving an Eton Ramblers cricket cap in its place).'

The son of the late Walter Robins, who played 19 Tests for England between 1929 and 1937 and chaired the national selection panel in the 1960s, thought little if at all about the cap until 1998, when his mother discovered what the moths had abandoned at the back of the airing cupboard in the family home in Suffolk. To assuage his guilt, Robins had it elaborately and expensively repaired by reputable antique fabric restorers in the Midlands and in time apologetically showed it to Mallett over lunch at a fish restaurant during a visit to Adelaide.

Delighted it had not perished and that Robins finally honoured his promise of the Eton Ramblers cap, which was nowhere to be found in 1972, Mallett magnanimously permitted Robins to keep the baggy green. However, when he later asked for it to be returned so he could present it to the Ayr Cricket Club in Scotland, with which he'd had such a happy association in his playing days, Mallett was shocked to learn Robins had sold it for an unknown sum.

Mallett had no idea what the cap would have fetched at auction, but with a wry smile conceded it would be many tens of thousands of dollars shy of the $425,000 Robins received from the sale of the cap Bradman had given him in 1956. At the time Bradman had returned to England to cover the Ashes for the *Daily Mail*.

Bradman had been particularly close to Walter Robins and recuperated at his home at Burnham, Essex after sustaining a flake fracture of his right ankle when his boot became caught in a foothold while he was bowling in the final Test at The Oval in August 1938. Such was their association that 10 years later Robins acted as the Australian Board of Control's liaison officer for Bradman's triumphant Invincibles tour. Robins, who captained England against New Zealand in 1937, died in 1968 aged 62.

While Mallett gave away other caps, three were bequeathed to his son, Ben. In his final match, the Centenary Test of 1980 at Lord's, Mallett was the only player wearing a cap bearing a date. Given that from the age of six he had dreamed of earning a baggy green, he thought it appropriate to wear the cap given to him for his first Test, also against England at The Oval in 1968.

MC

Bryce McGain debuted, aged 36, at Cape Town during the Australia versus South Africa Test. (Newspix)

CHAPTER 11

One Test in time

The knowledge that an elite cricketer has played just one Test match invariably elicits the gamut of opinions and emotions, and make no mistake: this is a very substantial cohort. At the start of the 2023–24 summer, 73 of Australia's 466 Test players had made a solitary appearance in the baggy green cap.

Indisputably some were unfortunate not to have played more often, circumstances conspiring against them at the most critical moment of their career, while conversely others were fortunate to have had their 30 hours of fame. Matters of selection are invariably complex and often subjective and emotive. As is the case in the middle, generally it is all about timing. All 73 men can attest to this in one way or another, and in the 21st century none more so than the highly accomplished South Australian swing bowler Chadd Sayers.

For five years from 2013 Sayers was on the selectors' short list and figured in their animated deliberations for season after season. Seemingly destined to be among the unluckiest of all peripheral players, at the age of 30 he was finally given his chance at Johannesburg in March 2018 and then only because he replaced Jackson Bird in the tour party and Mitchell Starc for the final match of a series forever besmirched by the sandpaper scandal.

Sayers is one of 11 players to have played a lone Test since 2008, and of this team only Will Pucovski remains in the minds of the selectors. If he can regain full health Pucovski can take heart from fellow opening batsman Chris Rogers and off spinner Nathan Hauritz, who both made spectacular returns to the international arena after long absences.

When this book was first published it was observed that Rogers, Hauritz and off spinner Dan Cullen, who had each appeared in one Test, remained hopeful they would be given another opportunity to don their baggy green caps. While Cullen fell from favour altogether, Hauritz returned four years to the month against New Zealand in November 2008 and played another 16 Tests. When he finally bowed out at the age of 28 in 2010 he could point to 63 wickets at 34.98, with two five-wicket hauls.

Rogers' resurgence was more remarkable. Seemingly destined to be a life member of the one-Test club, he was reinstated after five years and six months against England in July 2013 and flourished in 24 Tests over the next two years leading up to his 38th birthday. He finished with 2,015 Test runs at a very healthy 42.87, including four centuries against England and one against South Africa, when he contributed 107 of an innings of 216 in a heavy defeat at Port Elizabeth.

The gods did not shine so benevolently upon Sayers, who despite a celebrated career for South Australia could never defeat the naysayers who believed his stature and lack of pace restricted him. That he could probe and intimidate by swinging the ball in the manner of Bob Massie and Terry Alderman never placated his critics or earned him any favours. 'The knock on my pace was very frustrating,' Sayers said. 'I knew I couldn't get to 140 kph. It was hard to take. I'm not sure whether it was Darren Lehmann [coach] or Steve Smith [captain] who was so set on the 140 kph, but there it was.'

With 219 wickets, Sayers is the third-highest wicket taker for South Australia. Only legendary leg spinner Clarrie Grimmett, with 504 wickets between 1924–25 and 1940–41, and off spinner Ashley 'Rowdy' Mallett, with 344 wickets from 1967–68 to 1980–81, are ahead of him. Grimmett wore his baggy green on 37 occasions and Mallett 38 times.

While he would have relished more opportunities in the Test arena, Sayers is grateful that his patience and durability finally provided him with a crowning moment. 'It was a great achievement to play one Test,' he said.

'For me it was a dream come true. To get a chance to play was a privilege. The places cricket takes you, the people you meet. It is very special.'

Sayers was presented with his Test cap 452 by Adam Voges (cap 442) as the outraged cricket world digested news that Steve Smith, Australia's 45th Test match captain, along with vice-captain David Warner and Cameron Bancroft had been found guilty of bringing the game into disrepute and sent back to Australia. Furthermore, coach Darren Lehmann resigned.

Chad Sayers poses for the cameras ahead of his Test debut in 2018. (Newspix)

Voges, who was working as a media commentator, had three years earlier been summoned at the age of 35 to play the first of his 20 Tests in a remarkably productive 17 months that netted him 1,485 runs with five hundreds at the heady average of 61.9. Given only five days had elapsed since 'Sandpapergate' in Cape Town, Voges did his level best to normalise the situation. In offering his congratulations, he talked of a deep respect for the baggy green and called on Sayers to summon the skill and strength that had provided him with such an outstanding first-class career. 'There is no doubt what the boys went through and the scrutiny they were all under put a dampener on the week,' Sayers said. 'It was very difficult. Sad, really. But for me, my selection turned a bad week into a good one and I had the respect of everyone around me. The team took me under their wing.'

A former Bradman medallist in Adelaide district cricket and a runner-up to Ricky Ponting for Sheffield Shield player of the year, Sayers had the immense satisfaction of claiming the-then number one batsman in the world, A.B. de Villiers, as his first Test match wicket – and two deliveries later, Kagiso Rabada followed. 'Along with Jackson Bird I accepted we were the unlucky ones sitting behind [Mitchell] Starc, [Josh] Hazlewood, [Pat] Cummins, [James] Pattinson and [Peter] Siddle. That was understood, but always I tried to defy it all and I had good support from family and friends and especially Darren Berry. I always trained as hard and never gave up on my ambition.'

Remarkably, four of Sayers' South Australian contemporaries also experienced the range of complex emotions associated with a solitary Test match: Graham Manou (cap 411) deputised for keeper Brad Haddin at Birmingham in the 2009 Ashes, Peter George (416) was promoted versus India at Bangalore in 2010 and Callum Ferguson (445) and Joe Mennie (446) were summoned together against South Africa in Hobart in 2016.

Nine years before the uproar of Sandpapergate in Johannesburg, Victorian leg spinner Bryce McGain played his one Test match at Cape Town and was infamously mauled by A.B. de Villiers, Ashwell Prince and Jacques Kallis, who each scored a century.

Presented with baggy green 410 by captain Ricky Ponting (cap 366), McGain conceded eight sixes and 17 boundaries in one of the most demoralising initiations in the annals of the game, returning the figures of 0–149 from 18 overs. 'I'm incredibly proud of having played for Australia,' McGain said. He was a week shy of his 37th birthday and still not fully recovered from arm surgery five months earlier.

With just 90-minutes' notice from the team hierarchy, McGain became the oldest Australian debutant since fellow leg spinner Bob Holland against the West Indies in 1984–85 when he replaced Marcus North, who was in hospital on a drip suffering severe gastroenteritis. 'It was incredibly thrilling and I'm not ashamed at giving my best, giving it everything. Obviously it did not go as I had dreamt but I'm not ashamed. It all unfolded so quickly and the presentation of the cap was all a bit of a blur,' McGain said, 'but I do remember Ricky talked of the tradition of the cap and made mention of the time it had taken me to attain it. He said it was earned on merit and hoped I could wear it for longer. This was not to be, but neither was it the end. I continued to play for Victoria and had a short and enjoyable stint in country cricket with Essex.'

Ken Eastwood played one Test but is the proud owner of two baggy greens. (Image courtesy of Brydon Coverdale)

McGain continued playing club cricket into his 50s and became a recognised and well-regarded coach and mentor and thoughtful media commentator.

McGain and Sayers concur with former Victorian opening batsman Ken Eastwood that the egalitarianism of Australian cricket is celebrated whenever there is a gathering of men who have worn the baggy green, and as the powerbrokers of Cricket Australia and the Australian Cricketers' Association found more common ground in the late 1990s and into the new millennium, they pooled resources to formally recognise and celebrate the accomplishments of the country's elite cricketers at various ceremonies and functions.

'Whether you played one Test or 100 you are part of a group and always treated as an equal,' Eastwood said. 'I'm proud to be a member of such an elite group. It was a bonus as far as I am concerned. It is surprising what one Test can do for you. I am invited to various functions and dinners.' A remarkable sequence of events led to Eastwood's selection at the age of 35, a season after he had been feted as Victoria's highest run scorer with 744 at 41.33, while Bill Lawry's Australian team were on their torturous tour of India and South Africa. As Lawry, Keith Stackpole, Paul Sheahan and Ian Redpath were ahead of him in the pecking order, Eastwood never realistically expected to be summoned by the national selectors.

It may have been a home Test match, but Eastwood is the owner of two baggy greens that in all probability will be bequeathed to his daughters Jennifer and Catherine. He was given a choice of caps, but officials it seems were so distracted following the controversial sacking of Lawry as captain and player that no effort was made to reclaim the one he rejected.

Peter Allan and Ashley Woodcock both have three caps to show for their one outing in the baggy green. Allan received two for his selection in Bob Simpson's team for the famously acrimonious tour of the West Indies in 1964–65 and a third when chosen for his one appearance against England at the Gabba in December 1965, when Doug Walters announced his genius with 155 on debut.

Woodcock, who from a very young age intuitively understood that the baggy green epitomised the pinnacle for a cricketer, was presented with his first cap when chosen to open the batting against a World XI in 1971–72 following the cancellation of a scheduled tour by South Africa because of the threat of disruption by anti-apartheid protesters. Two years later he made his debut against New Zealand in front of his supportive home crowd at Adelaide Oval and then toured New Zealand. However, he did not perform well enough in the minor matches to dislodge either Redpath or Stackpole, who was at the end of a most entertaining 43-Test career.

Leg spinner Rex Sellers, who successfully reinvented himself as a batsman for South Australia, retired from the first-class game in 1967 just months before lean and elegant stroke player Woodcock made his first-class debut. Sellers, who had been born in the tiny siding of Valsad about 100 kilometres north of Mumbai, where his father was based as an engineer and bridge inspector in the Indian railways, had the satisfaction of making his only appearance at Kolkata in October 1964. Although rain ruined the match, his selection provided some compensation for the frustration of missing so much of the preceding England tour because of surgery to his spinning finger.

Members of the Australian team before leaving for the 1974 tour of New Zealand, including debutant Ashley Woodcock (third from the left). (Newspix)

The egalitarianism of which Eastwood is so proud is echoed by Kim Hughes, Australia's 37th captain and a thrilling batsman who polarised the Australian cricket community when for two tumultuous summers he forsook the baggy green and played in rebel colours in South Africa. 'It is noticeable at big reunions of past players that there is no pecking order. If you have the baggy green you are on the team whether you have played one Test or 50. I'm very proud of that,' Hughes said.

Despite the turbulence of the time he served, on just a single occasion in 28 Tests as Australian captain did Hughes lead a player chosen only once for his country. In his first match as captain deputising for the injured Graham Yallop in the second Test with Pakistan at Perth in

March 1979, he oversaw the debut of Yallop's replacement, Victorian Jeff Moss. Such was the acrimony of proceedings it was soon forgotten that Australia prospered by seven wickets and that Moss made a useful contribution to the victory.

Jeff Moss played a single Test and a sole ODI for Australia in 1979. (Newspix)

Pakistani paceman Sikander Bakht was run out by bowler Alan Hurst while backing up, and Andrew Hilditch was given out handled the ball after retrieving a wayward return and handing the ball to prickly Sarfraz Nawaz. These moments of high drama obscured the fact Moss scored 22 and an undefeated 38 to win some encouraging notices. With Allan Border, Moss added 81 in an unbroken fourth-wicket partnership and had the satisfaction of leg glancing guileful medium pacer Mudassar Nazar for the single, which enabled the Australians to square the two-match contest after they had lost heavily in the opening Test in Melbourne.

Moss appeared in one match at the 1979 World Cup in England but was not chosen for the Test tour of India under Hughes later in the year and did not again play for Australia. Be that as it may, Hughes tips his cap to Moss, who rejoices at being treated as one of the family whenever those privileged to have worn the baggy green gather to talk of salad days.

MC

Mitchell Starc and winemaker/wool grower Grant Burge with Merino ram Achilles at the Adelaide Oval to promote the Flock to Baggy Green initiative. (Newspix)

CHAPTER 12

Wool promotions: from flock to baggy green

In 2012 it became apparent that the cap was indeed still relevant commercially. Corporations saw a financial benefit in being associated with the cap and the golden fleece from which it's made, even if the cap couldn't be used as a billboard.

The Australian menswear label M.J. Bale was the official tailor to the Australian cricket team. As one of Cricket Australia's newest and smallest sponsors, they were invisible to the general public as they were not named on bats, pitch or outfield. A campaign was devised to raise awareness of the company and its link to cricket.

A plan was hatched whereby turf from the Sydney Cricket Ground, the site of Australia's greatest cricketing successes, was regrown on the property of wool grower Bill Mitchell at Guyra, near Armidale in New England. This turf was grazed upon by his merino sheep and the superfine wool from the flock sent to Italy to be woven into fine yarn. This was then used by M.J. Bale for the suits worn by the Australian team.

The campaign and video called 'Grazed on Greatness' won six awards at the Cannes Lions Festival of Creativity, the international advertising industry's equivalent of the Academy Awards.

Australian Wool Innovation chair Colette Garnsey presented Cricket Australia chairman Earl Eddings the next era of baggy green cloth in Adelaide in 2018. (Image courtesy of Richard Smith, Australian Wool Innovation)

The campaign was a commercial success, with suit sales up 520 per cent. While the baggy green is made from woollen flannel, what's the connection?

A letter was dispatched to Bill Mitchell in early 2013 congratulating them on the innovative promotion, and politely suggesting the baggy green be made from Australian superfine merino wool and the industry could garnish visibility by association. In 2018 sheepcentral.com proudly announced that more than 100 wool growers were participating in the Australian Wool Innovation (AWI) project. These growers donated about 300 kilograms of wool to be made into the next batch of baggy greens, with each grower receiving a sample of the finished product as a keepsake.

In December 2018 the AWI chairman, Colette Garnsey OAM, presented Cricket Australia's chairman Earl Eddings with the next era of baggy green cloth. The presentation at Adelaide Oval during the Test secured wide coverage. The AWI release stated 'Woolgrowers donate the next 100 years of baggy greens' then declared: 'All donors to the project have been placed on a map of Australia on the dedicated website www.flocktobaggygreen.com.au where *From Flock to Baggy Green* by renowned cricket writer Gideon Haigh outlines the strong and lasting bonds between cricket and wool.'

AWI general manager of operations Nigel Gosse outlined that the work with Cricket Australia was part of AWI's commitment to its fibre advocacy program. 'Flock to Baggy Green has created a lasting legacy from the wool growers of Australia to Australian cricket, adding to the history and provenance of one of our nation's most significant sporting icons,' he explained. 'Cricket-loving wool growers from the outback to the coast, from large pastoral holdings to small family businesses, have all answered the call to help grow the Baggy Green. All have donated some of the natural fibre they grow with passion to help make our most sacred sporting icon.

'At AWI our role is to increase the long-term profitability of Australian wool growers and to advocate for the natural fibre domestically and overseas. This fabric has been grown on more than 450 properties across Australia and donated by cricket-loving wool growers, which adds to the history and provenance of one of our nation's most significant sporting icons. The presentation creates a lasting legacy from the wool growers of Australia to Australian cricket.'

Australian Test cricket debutants of the modern era, including Alex Carey, play in caps made from wool from the AWI project. (Alamy)

The Flock to Baggy Green project combined the Australian wool industry, Cricket Australia and Kookaburra to create special baggy green cloth made from wool donated from across Australia. Earl Eddings said the project will continue to build the meaning of the baggy green cap for Australian cricketers: 'Australian cricket is shared and loved across Australia. Likewise, the Australian wool industry has played a pivotal part in the Australian way of life, so to combine the two gives the Baggy Green Cap fantastic meaning for future Australian Test cricketers. Our future Test cricketers can wear their caps with pride, knowing wool growers from around the country have contributed to its creation.'

From Flock to Baggy Green *by Gideon Haigh, published by Australian Wool Innovation Limited 2018. (Image courtesy of Michael Fahey)*

In total just over 400 wool growers donated wool to the project, with the total volume coming to around 500 kilograms. Each wool grower received a sample of the finished fabric as a memento of their contribution to Australian cricket. One such donor was Grant Burge, renowned winemaker and wool grower from the Barossa Valley in South Australia. He knew most people would know him for his wine but asserted that his family had always been in sheep. He offered a whole bale, as he is a cricket lover and long-term sponsor of South Australia. 'I love my Test cricket and understand the reverence for the baggy green, so I thought I'd put my hand up as a lover of Test cricket.'

To further document and cement the link between sheep, wool and the baggy green, historian and author Gideon Haigh was commissioned to write the book *From Flock to Baggy Green* (Australian Wool Innovation), which was released in 2018. Gideon advised it was 'a small addition to baggy green lore'.

MF

Shane Warne announced in early 2020 he would auction off his cap to raise funds for the bushfire appeal. (Newspix)

CHAPTER 13

Lap of honour

Conjecture that the baggy green cap would lose relevance in the age of franchise cricket was dispelled when coveted cap 350 famously circumnavigated Australia out of sight of its legendary benefactor Shane Warne. Furthermore, thousands of Australians the length and breadth of the country queued for the opportunity to pull on white gloves and gingerly examine the cap worn for 15 years by the peerless leg spinner.

Universally and affectionately known as 'Warnie', the most charismatic cricketer of his era magnanimously gifted his cap to a nation in severe shock following the devastating Black Summer bushfires of 2019 and 2020. A much-loved if polarising cricketer, Warne became a persuasive voice and his cap a powerful symbol for the Australian Red Cross disaster relief and recovery fund, which had been established to assist the thousands of Australians emotionally and financially devastated by the terrifying infernos.

The online auction for the cap captured the imagination of the public and sparked frenetic bidding from collectors, investors and dreamers alike until Matt Comyn, the chief executive officer of the Commonwealth Bank, a long-standing and staunch sponsor of Australian cricket, had the final word. Comyn claimed the prize on behalf of the nation with a bid of $1,007,500, a startling

Shane Warne hands over his baggy green cap to Matt Comyn, Commonwealth Bank CEO, at the MCG. The bank paid $1,007,500 for the cap. (Newspix)

$582,500 more than the previous record paid in 2003 for Sir Donald Bradman's 1948 Invincibles cap 124.

Warne was as astonished as professional valuers and memorabilia dealers and immediately took to social media to say: 'You have blown me away with your generosity and this was way beyond my expectations.' Well known for his generosity of spirit and quiet philanthropy, the success of the auction was another measure of Warne's popularity and relevance 13 years after the last of his 145 Test matches and seven years after his direct playing association with all formats of the game had ended.

Comyn ensured the cap of the people's cricketer was indeed shared with the people by immediately announcing it would be donated to and permanently displayed at the Bradman Museum and International Cricket Hall of Fame at Bowral in the Southern Highlands of New South Wales. 'I want to thank and commend Shane for giving up one of his most cherished possessions for such an important cause,' Comyn said. 'He has demonstrated the same Aussie spirit we are seeing across the country, with acts of generosity and dedication throughout this disaster and communities rallying to support each other.'

Furthermore, Comyn signed off on a national tour for the cap under the banner 'The Comm Bank Baggy Green Tour – Supporting bushfire affected communities'. Packed in a bulky 40-kilogram showcase and accompanied by chaperones and appropriate security, baggy green 350 began its lap of honour at the Big Bash League final between the Sydney Sixers and Melbourne Stars at the Sydney Cricket Ground on 8 February, as many fires raged out of control. It visited Commonwealth Bank branches, parks, ovals, street fairs, clubs, family fun days in all six states and the Northern Territory and was at the Melbourne Cricket Ground in March when a world-record crowd of 86,174 witnessed Australia overpower India in the Women's T20 World Cup final.

The most poignant visit was to the town of Batemans Bay on the south coast of New South Wales, which seven weeks earlier had been surrounded by raging infernos that had compelled residents and hundreds of holidaymakers to flee to the beach for their safety. Locals and visitors gathered at the town's street fair on 19 February and, exhausted by shared stories of suffering and survival, sought distraction by learning about the baggy green cap and Warne's relationship with his fabled headwear. The tour had only just left the mainland for Elizabeth Street in Hobart when it was curtailed because of the worsening COVID-19 pandemic.

That the auction and subsequent tour of the cap garnered such media attention provided Warne with a platform to explain his complex relationship with his baggy green. Certainly he had been deeply offended when on isolated occasions his affection for the cap had been publicly questioned. 'I always cherished the baggy green cap, and it sat alongside me in every dressing room I played in around the world,' he declared for Mike Coward's *Warne Worn: The baggy green that rallied Australia* (Churchill Press, 2020), a publication for the Bradman Museum celebrating his magnanimity, his cap, the tour and the museum.

'I always wore it in the first session of Test matches. But I always believed I didn't have to wear the baggy green to say how much I loved to play for Australia. I was just as proud to be an Australian player in my white floppy hat. It is just the misuse of the cap I didn't like and didn't respect,' Warne said, hinting at the directive of captain Steve Waugh to wear the baggy green on a visit to the Wimbledon tennis championship in 2001. 'I don't buy into all that stuff they go on about the fabric of the cap, all that hysteria. But I have always loved the cap and what it stands for. Always cherished it.'

His cap was formally presented to the Bradman Museum and therefore to the Australian cricket community on a red-letter day on the nation's cricket and cultural calendar: 27 August, the date of Bradman's birth in 1908. Dr Maurice Newman, the-then chairman of the Bradman Foundation, accepted the grand donation from Comyn to the warm applause of local dignitaries including senior police, rural fire service and Wingecarribee Shire Council representatives. They more than most in attendance appreciated Warne's gesture and generosity.

Nine months earlier, in Christmas week 2019, their services had been needed to pool resources as fires reached the Southern Highlands. The Bradman Oval, adjacent to the museum, was a designated safe haven for residents fleeing the nearby villages of Balmoral, Bargo, Hill Top, Colo Vale and Yerrinbool. At the height of the local emergency as many as 50 people a day sought sanctuary and made use of the amenities at the oval and its pavilion. Some exercised their dogs and smaller farm animals within the white pickets.

The Bradman Museum's 'Baggy Green: The Story of an Australian Icon' display in 2020. (Image courtesy of AJ Moran Photography)

Barely three weeks later the region was seriously threatened again when the devastating and long-running Currowan fire attacked from the south, destroying houses and property at Wingello, Bundanoon and Kangaroo

Valley. The nation was ablaze for nine months from June 2019 until the final fires were extinguished on 4 March 2020. Two years later to the day Warne died of a heart attack while holidaying in Thailand. He was aged 52. Bradman had died in 2001 at the age of 92.

To coincide with Warne's benefaction and in association with the Commonwealth Bank, the museum established the permanent exhibition 'Baggy Green: The Story of an Australian Icon'. That it showcases the caps of two of the world's foremost cricketers added lustre to the institution. Both Sir Donald Bradman and Warne were among the five cricketers of the 20th century chosen for the millennium edition of *Wisden Cricketers' Almanack*.

Born 61 years apart, they met formally at least once: at Bradman's home at the time of his 90th birthday in 1998, when 28-year-old Warne had the honour of introducing his friend and nemesis Sachin Tendulkar. As it is said in India, Tendulkar had travelled to Adelaide 'to wish' Bradman on the auspicious occasion. While there was much media speculation about the topics of conversation between the game's peerless batsmen, adherents of the arcane art of leg-spin bowling pondered the likely exchanges between Bradman and Warne.

Six years into a celebrated Test career that was to last to 2007 and realise a phenomenal 708 wickets, Warne was afforded the rare chance to seek Bradman's views on leg-spin bowling. Earlier in his career on coir matting at Bowral, Bradman had often claimed wickets with his leg breaks, but as his batting flourished and brought him international renown his bowling became an incidental pursuit. Whenever pressed to discuss his bowling Bradman, in a self-deprecating manner, said he was content to 'leave it to those who knew what they were doing'. In a 52-Test career that saw him accumulate 6,996 runs at 99.94, he delivered just 164 balls and captured two wickets – those of West Indian Ivan Barrow in 1930–31 and England's Walter Hammond in 1932–33 – while conceding 72 runs.

Warne always insisted his pride in playing for Australia was all-consuming whether he was under the baggy green, a white floppy hat or the green and gold skullcap bearing cricket's coat of arms. This was self-evident on countless occasions throughout his illustrious career and notably at the 50-over world cup in England in 1999, when successive virtuoso performances against South Africa and Pakistan earned Australia the title.

Nearly two decades later Warne, an insightful if garrulous television pundit, learned that his man of the match achievement in the remarkable tied semi-final against South Africa was seared into the memory of Marnus Labuschagne, the wearer of baggy green cap 455. Born in the mining city of Klerksdorp in the North-West province of South Africa in June 1994, Labuschagne migrated with his family at the age of eight and realised an ambition to play Test cricket for Australia against Pakistan in Dubai in October 2018.

A 1948 cap that is part of the Bradman Museum's collection. Warne's cap joined the collection on Bradman's birthday, 27 August 2020. (Image courtesy of AJ Moran Photography)

'I grew up knowing of the existence of a baggy green cap but it was a South African one, not an Australian one,' Labuschagne conceded. 'I was only about five but I remember watching the 1999 World Cup on television and vividly recall the famous run out of Allan Donald and the disappointment that followed when South Africa lost to Australia in such a way. I also remember watching the next world cup in South Africa from afar as the family had just moved to Australia.'

As he abandoned his mother tongue of Afrikaans and embraced Australia and its cricket and customs, Labuschagne soon learned of the

Teammates congratulate bowler Cameron Green and fielder Marnus Labuschagne after the latter's catch that dismissed West Indian captain Kraigg Brathwaite during the Gabba Test in January 2024. (Alamy)

lore associated with the fabled Aussie baggy green cap. At the age of 20 and just weeks after making his first-class debut for Queensland against South Australia, he first set eyes on the genuine article when nominated as the substitute fieldsman for Australia at the second Test with India at the Gabba in December 2014. To his unbridled delight captain Steve Smith, perhaps with an eye to the immediate future, insisted he be included in the team celebration of the hard-fought, four-wicket victory and allowed him to join the singing of the team song.

It was a thrilling introduction to the Australian dressing room for Labuschagne, who had taken a close-in catch from the bowling of Nathan Lyon and observed the joy of paceman Josh Hazlewood making his Test debut with baggy green cap 440. Forty-six months later in Dubai it was Labuschagne who was feted and welcomed into the fold and ceremoniously handed baggy green 455 cap by Mike Hussey, the prominent owner of cap 393.

Labuschagne confessed the cap is his one irreplaceable possession, and at home in Brisbane it is locked in a safe. On tour he carries it in a backpack, unwilling to take the risk of packing it in his coffin or other checked baggage. 'My baggy green represents everything I dreamed of doing as a kid and it's the culmination of thousands of hours in the nets training to be the best cricketer I can be,' Labuschagne said. 'It's been all around the world with me and soaked into the green wool is hundreds and hundreds of hours of sweat, tears, sunscreen, change room celebrations and camaraderie.'

The security and condition of the cap is a constant concern to all Australian players, who are generally reluctant to wash their priceless headwear for fear of damaging the wool and sacrosanct cricket coat of arms.

Many years after his Test debut against India in Perth in January 2008, opening batsman Chris Rogers still breaks into a cold sweat recalling his first day in baggy green 399. Ceremoniously presented to him by recently retired opener Justin Langer, bearer of baggy green 354, Rogers soon discovered his head was too big for the cap, which led to troublesome headaches. To the horror of his new teammates, Rogers used scissors to try to loosen and stretch the cap but instead ripped it badly. 'What have you done?' exclaimed his opening partner Phil Jaques, possessor of baggy green 395.

It took five years, but to his immense relief Rogers eventually atoned for an inauspicious Test debut with a splitting headache and a borrowed cap and played solidly in 24 more Tests for 2015 runs at 42.9, with five centuries – in brand-new baggy green 399.

MC

Endnotes

INTRODUCTION

1. http://www.dfat.gov.au/facts/coat_of_arms.html.
2. Marylebone Cricket Club press release, 22 September 2003.
3. Lord's Press release, 22 September 2003.
4. Marcus Williams and Gordon Phillips, *The Wisden Book of Cricket Memorabilia*, Lennard Publishing, 1990. Appendix, page 315: 'The aggressive bidding of the Antipodeans was enjoyed by all at the MCC Bicentenary auction, glowering away at each other.'

2. THE ROAD TO THE BAGGY GREEN

5. Peter Sharpham, *Sporting Traditions*, May 1994.
6. Richard Cashman, 'Branding of Australian Cricket: Culture, Commerce, Cricket and the baggy green cap', *Sporting Traditions*, November 2006.
7. Jack Pollard, *The Pictorial History of Australian Cricket*, J.M. Dent, 1983.
8. Ibid.
9. Richard Cashman, *The 'Demon' Spofforth*, University of New South Wales Press, 1990.
10. Philip Derriman, 'The Green and Gold – 100 Years Young', *Wisden Cricketers' Almanack Australia*, 1999.
11. David Frith, *Pageant of Cricket*, Macmillan, 1987.
12. Richard Bouwman, *Glorious Innings: Treasures from the Melbourne Cricket Club Collection*, Hutchinson Australia, 1987.
13. Pollard, *The Pictorial History of Australian Cricket*.

14. Newspaper cutting, New South Wales Cricket Association library.

15. Hugh Field, *History of the Melbourne Cricket Club*, unpublished manuscript, Melbourne Cricket Club library.

3. THE GUM-TREE GREEN AND GOLD

16. I was a shareholder of and consultant to Legends.

17. A limited edition of 500, 'The Pride of the Baggy Green', was signed by Steve Waugh and contained an actual swatch of baggy green material with the coat of arms, supplied by the cap's maker Albion Hat & Cap Co Pty Ltd.

18. Philip Derriman, 'The Green and Gold – 100 Years Young', *Wisden Cricketers' Almanack Australia*, 1999. This is quoted from a letter dated 25 May 1910.

19. Malcolm Conn, 'Australia's greats to dine out on good memories', *The Australian*, 23 December 1999.

20. Emma John, 'Classless at New Road', *Wisden Cricket Monthly*, June 2000.

21. Philip Derriman, 'The Green and Gold – 100 Years Young'.

22. Mike Coward, 'So proud to be capped and numbered', *The Australian*, 12 July 2003.

23. Steve Waugh, 'If the cap's fixed and still fits I'll wear it', *The Daily Telegraph*, 21 November 2002.

24. Tony Stephens, 'A baggy green for Invincible Bill, and that youngster Brett', *SMH*, 11 July 2003.

25. Tony Stephens, 'Wearing of the green bags a place in our soul', *SMH*, 12 July 2003.

26. Minutes and citations were supplied by Gideon Haigh for his book with David Frith, *Inside Story: Unlocking Australian cricket's archive*, News Custom Printing, 2007.

27. Frank Laver Collection, Melbourne Cricket Club Museum.

28. Peter Sharpman, *Charlie Macartney: Cricket's 'Governor-General'*, Walla Walla Press, 2004.

29. Philip Derriman, 'The cap fits, so wear it properly', *SMH*, 10 July 1997.

30. Philip Derriman, 'The Green and Gold: 100 Years Young', *Wisden Cricketer's Almanack Australia 1999*, Hardie Grant Publishing, 1999.

31. Ibid.

32. Conversation with Ross Barrat of Albion.

33. David Sygall, 'Baggy green gets a personalised touch', *SMH*, 17 November 2002.

34. Richard Cashman, *Sport in the National Imagination*, Walla Walla Press, 2002.

35. Gideon Haigh, *The Big Ship: Warwick Armstrong and the making of modern cricket*, Text Publishing, 2001.

36. State Library South Australia, 'Don Bradman', www.slsa.gov.au/bradman/cap.

37. Viv Jenkins, *The Baggy Green: World series to world champions*, New Holland Publishers, 1998.

38. Only 24 caps were made, one for each player, one for each state association and the ACB and several for museums: Malcolm Conn, *Inside Edge*, February 2000.

39. Unknown, 'If the old Aussie cap fits, wear it', *The Daily Telegraph*, 2 January 2000.

40. 1905 Australian Cricket Team, 15 unnumbered cards issued by Snider & Abrahams, 1905.

41. A poster signed by 16 of the 19 captains listed was valued by Michael Fahey in 'What's it worth?', a column in the Legends publication *The Sporting Collector*, edition no. 4, 2002.

42. Cricket Australia, Re-branding Australian Cricket, 2002–03 annual report.

43. A.J.M. Hewitt, 'Cricket caps, once a symbol, are not in the fashion these days', *Playfair Cricket Monthly*, February 1971.

44. Emma John, 'Classless at New Road'.

45. Malcolm Conn, 'Green with envy', *Inside Edge*, February 2000.

46. Rohit Brijnath, 'The Importance of Rituals', *Sportstar*, 10–16 November 2001

47. Tony Stephens, 'Wearing of the green bags a place in our soul', *SMH*, 12 July 2003.

4. COLLECTORS

48. Marcus Williams and Gordon Phillips, *The Wisden Book of Cricket Memorabilia*, Lennard Publishing, 1990.

49. Ibid.

50. The Centenary Port collection produced in Australia depicted the participants in the first Test. Subsequent testimonial ports exist for Dennis Lillee and Doug Walters.

51. Wesley Walters's *From the Hill*, a signed print of the painting depicting Bradman's 100th hundred. Marketed by the New South Wales Cricket Association in the 1970s, it was produced as a limited edition of 1,250 as was the John Bloomfield painting *Caught Marsh Bowled Lillee* from the 1977 Centenary Test.

52. Melbourne Cricket Club, 'Museums', www.mcc.org.au, accessed 1 August 2007.

53. Conversations with Richard Ferguson, manager of Exhibitions and Collections, Museums Department, Melbourne Cricket Club, and David Studham, librarian at the Melbourne Cricket Club.

54. State Library of South Australia, 'Don Bradman', www.slsa.sa.gov.au/bradman/cap.htm, accessed March 2007.

55. Email correspondence with David Frith, June 2007.

56. James Cockington, 'Money "Collect"', *SMH*, 14 June 2006.

5. VALUES

57. Phillip Koch, 'Past for Sale', *The Sunday Telegraph*, 6 December 1998.

58. Ibid.

59. Unknown, '$45,000 for Test original', *The Australian*, 5 December 1998.

6. THE TAJ MAHAL OF BAGGY GREENS

60. The tax was introduced by the Howard government on 1 July 2000 as a 10 per cent impost on virtually all service and trade transactions within Australia.

61. Angus Fontaine (ed.), 'Farewell Sir Don' from 'Bradman: a Tribute', *Inside Edge*, 2001.

62. Rod Nicholson, 'Bring Bradman's baggy cap home', *The Daily Telegraph* (Sydney), 21 May 2003.

63. Unknown, 'Sale of Bradman's cap fails to end mystery', *The Age*, 24 June 2003.

64. 'Bradman memorabilia sells at record price', interview with Christie's cricket expert Andrew McVinish, *AM*, ABC Radio, 25 June 2003.

65. 'Baggy green beggars', *Media Watch*, 7 January 2003, www.abc.net.au/mediawatch/transcipts/s896810.htm.

66. Rod Nicholson, 'Baggy green coming home', *Herald Sun*, 30 June 2003.

67. Unknown, 'Dons cap earns $425,000', *The Border Mail*, 1 July 2003.

68. Coffs Harbour City Council media officer Ian Cameron, 'Cricket icon adds to Coffs Coast allure', Coffs Harbour City Council media release, 2 October 2003.

69. 'Past and present cricket treasures feature in Travelex Cricket Roadshow', Travelex press release, 9 January 2004.

70. Cricket Australia, 'Travelex Cricket Roadshow rides again', *Insight*, February–April 2003.

71. dawn.com (the website of Pakistan's most widely circulated English language newspaper), 'Bradman's cap leaves collector with big tax bill', 10 September 2003.

72. Unknown, 'GST capped at $42,500', *SMH*, 9 September 2003.

73. Bronwyn Hurell, 'A gift to us: The Don's cap comes home', *The Advertiser*, 25 November 2004.

7. VARIATIONS AND ODDITIES

74. Christie's Australia Cricket Auction, 27 June 1999, #454, estimate $4,000 to $6,000. Passed in.

75. Australian War Memorial, 'Stolen Years: Australian prisoners of war – Prisoners in Germany', in Hohenfels, P02071.029, www.awm.gov/stolenyears/ww2/germany/story3.html.

76. Auction, 8 December 2001, item # 275, worn by Cec Pepper, Reserve £350 to £500, sold for £330.

77. Offered in Boxshalls #4 sale, 12 May 2000, item #171.

78. Viv Jenkins, *The Baggy Green: World Series to world champions*, New Holland Publishers, 1998.

79. Unknown, 'Just for a second, Waugh the hard man cracks', *SMH*, 22 October 2002.

Acknowledgements

This edition of *The Baggy Green* is a complete revision and update of the 2008 release.

As soon as I began the original project I realised very little research existed and that my frustration was shared by others in auction houses and museums.

I would like to thank the following people: David Wells at the Bradman Museum in Bowral, who was a cheerful source of much information; Stephen Gibbs, who provided a great treasure of photocopies of articles and caps references; Cricket Australia's Samantha Burn, Peter Young, Philip Pope and Kelly Sedgeway all provided assistance, as did David Steinhardt from Velocity Brand Management, who manages licensing for Cricket Australia; Colin Clowes, the librarian at Cricket New South Wales; Brian Clinton, who painted the Art of Bradman portraits; and Gideon Haigh, who provided information from the Cricket Australia minutes and offered learned theories when we were stumped about certain issues.

Journalists Ian Heads and Philip Derriman for their guidance; Richard Cashman and Peter Sharpham for their groundbreaking work on Australian sporting history, especially as the co-authors of the article 'Symbols, Emblems, Colours and Names' (*Sport in the National Imagination*, Walla Walla Press,

2002); and Roger Page of Roger Page Cricket Books for help to track down required publications.

Ross Barrat, formerly of Albion, who generously spent a large amount of time providing details about the history of the cap and its manufacture.

Staff at the Melbourne Cricket Club: librarian David Studham and the former manager of exhibitions Richard Ferguson; and Jed Smith at the Australian Sports Museum.

In England I received help from James Greenfield of Yorkshire Cricket Archives; Glenys Williams, Marylebone Cricket Club archivist and historian at Lord's; Neil Robinson at the Marylebone Cricket Club library; Keith Hayhurst from the Old Trafford Museum; and Sue Wilson at Lancashire County Cricket Club.

In Australia assistance came from: Cheryl Crilly of the National Museum of Australia; Geoff Havercroft and Steve Hall of the Western Australian Cricket Association; Suzy Russell from the State Library of South Australia; and Bernard Whimpress at the South Australian Cricket Association.

Baggy green collectors David Frith (UK), John Kirkness, Harry Wzola, Neil Mumford, Jason Brooks and Craig Hawkins.

Max Dunbar of Christie's in Britain; Mike Down of Boundary Books; Tom Thompson, who provided auction results for Lawson's and Cromwell's; Charles Leski of Leski Auctions; John Mullock of Mullock's Specialist Auctioneers and Valuers; Michael Treloar Antiquarian Booksellers; Trevor Vennett-Smith from T. Vennett-Smith Auctions; David Boxshall of Boxshalls; Graham Budd of Graham Budd Auctions; Tim Knight of Knights Auctioneers; David Lee-Steere of Framous Memorabilia stores; Brett Corrick, general manager and director of ISC-Sport; John Fordham of The Fordham Company, which manages Mark Taylor; Brenton Siggs, who helped with information regarding the service's team; Steve Cashman and the members of the Cricket Memorabilia Society; local collectors and enthusiasts Peter Schofield, Neil Mumford, Rod Mater, Thos Hodgson and Derrick Townsend; and Kate Boyd, Ted a'Beckett's daughter.

I am grateful for the time Guy Masters, Katie Fahey and Victor Yoog spent assisting with the earlier edition,

Our 2008 editor, Mark Ray, provided a unique pool of literary, photographic and cricketing experience. My co-author Mike Coward brought a wealth of cricket knowledge, sober judgement and wise counsel.

Our 2008 publisher Ronald Cardwell was invaluable with his wealth of cricket knowledge.

Luke West and the team at Rockpool Publishing for their enthusiasm in reinvigorating the book and encouraging us to explore the changes in the last 15 years and the growth of women's cricket, and examining the relevancy of the baggy green in 2023.

MF

About the authors and contributors

Michael Fahey has been one of the major players in the sports memorabilia scene for much of the past 40 years. He was born in 1962 and graduated from Sydney University with an Economics degree after attending St Ignatius College, Riverview.

Michael has been trading and valuing sports memorabilia since 1993 and sold the four match balls from the Rugby World Cup 2003 final for a world-record price for rugby memorabilia of $250,000. He is now the official valuer to ASM, Rugby Australia Archives, the Sydney Cricket Ground, Bradman and New Zealand rugby museums, the New Zealand Sports Hall of Fame and is the approved valuer of the Commonwealth government's Cultural Gifts Program.

In 2008 Michael co-wrote *The History of the Baggy Green* and spoke on it in the Long Room at Lord's. The book was awarded runner-up at the Australian Cricket Society's Literary Award 2008–09 and the Award for Excellence at the Cricket Memorabilia Society in 2009. He is also the founder and administrator of a number of sports history Facebook pages, including History of the Wallaby Jersey and Cricket remembered. In 2016 he co-presented the seminar 'Protecting the Legacy' for New Zealand rugby on the All Blacks jersey in 2016.

He and Jed Smith of the Australian Sports Museum formed the Sports Museum Network of Australia and New Zealand, a body for museum professionals. So far five seminars for this group have been held across Australia.

Michael co-wrote with Mark Cashman *The Official History of the Wallabies Jersey: The journey to find Wallaby Gold* (Sports Memorabilia Australia, 2023).

Mike Coward is a senior freelance journalist and one of Australia's most-experienced cricket writers and commentators, having covered the game throughout the world since 1972.

Formerly chief cricket writer for *The Sydney Morning Herald* and *The Advertiser* (Adelaide), he was the cricket columnist for *The Australian* for 20 years to 2011. An experienced public speaker and compère, he has broadcast the game for radio and television and written, ghosted or edited 15 cricket books. He was the interviewer for each of the eight programs in ABC Television's *Cricket History* series and for the extensive archive at the Bradman Museum and International Cricket Hall of Fame.

Peter Sharpham was born in Sydney in 1945. A keen rugby and cricket player in his youth, he earned a master's degree in sports history at Illinois State University in 1980. He has collected photographs, programs and other ephemera since he was 12. His interests include surfing, playing masters cricket, mining opals at Coober Pedy, art history and classical music. He has written two cricket biographies and one tour book, and is a member of the Sydney-based Company of Cricket Scribes. He has two sons, Leif and Eric.